INTRODUCING
ISSUES WITH
OPPOSING
VIEWPOINTS®

The
Patriot Act

Lauri S. Friedman, *Book Editor*

GREENHAVEN PRESS
A part of Gale, Cengage Learning

GALE
CENGAGE Learning

Detroit • New York • San Francisco • New Haven, Conn • Waterville, Maine • London

Christine Nasso, *Publisher*
Elizabeth Des Chenes, *Managing Editor*

For more information, contact:
Greenhaven Press
27500 Drake Rd.
Farmington Hills, MI 48331-3535
Or you can visit our Internet site at gale.cengage.com

LIBRARY OF CONGRESS CATALOGING-IN-PUBLICATION DATA

The Patriot Act / Lauri S. Friedman, book editor.
   p. cm. — (Introducing issues with opposing viewpoints)
  Includes bibliographical references and index.
  ISBN 978-0-7377-4172-8 (hardcover)
1. United States. Uniting and Strengthening America by Providing Appropriate
Tools Required to Intercept and Obstruct Terrorism (USA PATRIOT ACT) Act of
2001—Juvenile literature. 2. Terrorism—United States—Prevention—Juvenile
literature. 3. National security—Law and legislation—United States—Juvenile
literature. 4. Civil rights—United States—Juvenile literature. 5. War on
Terrorism, 2001—Law and legislation—United States—Juvenile literature.
I. Friedman, Lauri S.
  KF9430.P375 2009
  345.73'02—dc22
                                              2008040081

Printed in the United States of America
1 2 3 4 5 6 7 12 11 10 09 08

Contents

Chapter 3: Who Is Threatened by the Patriot Act?

Foreword

Indulging in a wide spectrum of ideas, beliefs, and perspectives is a critical cornerstone of democracy. After all, it is often debates over differences of opinion, such as whether to legalize abortion, how to treat prisoners, or when to enact the death penalty, that shape our society and drive it forward. Such diversity of thought is frequently regarded as the hallmark of a healthy and civilized culture. As the Reverend Clifford Schutjer of the First Congregational Church in Mansfield, Ohio, declared in a 2001 sermon, "Surrounding oneself with only like-minded people, restricting what we listen to or read only to what we find agreeable is irresponsible. Refusing to entertain doubts once we make up our minds is a subtle but deadly form of arrogance." With this advice in mind, Introducing Issues with Opposing Viewpoints books aim to open readers' minds to the critically divergent views that comprise our world's most important debates.

Introducing Issues with Opposing Viewpoints simplifies for students the enormous and often overwhelming mass of material now available via print and electronic media. Collected in every volume is an array of opinions that captures the essence of a particular controversy or topic. Introducing Issues with Opposing Viewpoints books embody the spirit of nineteenth-century journalist Charles A. Dana's axiom: "Fight for your opinions, but do not believe that they contain the whole truth, or the only truth." Absorbing such contrasting opinions teaches students to analyze the strength of an argument and compare it to its opposition. From this process readers can inform and strengthen their own opinions, or be exposed to new information that will change their minds. Introducing Issues with Opposing Viewpoints is a mosaic of different voices. The authors are statesmen, pundits, academics, journalists, corporations, and ordinary people who have felt compelled to share their experiences and ideas in a public forum. Their words have been collected from newspapers, journals, books, speeches, interviews, and the Internet, the fastest growing body of opinionated material in the world.

Introducing Issues with Opposing Viewpoints shares many of the well-known features of its critically acclaimed parent series, Opposing Viewpoints. The articles are presented in a pro/con format, allowing readers to absorb divergent perspectives side by side. Active reading questions preface each viewpoint, requiring the student to approach the material thoughtfully and carefully. Useful charts, graphs, and cartoons supplement each article. A thorough introduction provides readers with crucial background on an issue. An annotated bibliography points the reader toward articles, books, and Web sites that contain additional information on the topic. An appendix of organizations to contact contains a wide variety of charities, nonprofit organizations, political groups, and private enterprises that each hold a position on the issue at hand. Finally, a comprehensive index allows readers to locate content quickly and efficiently.

Introducing Issues with Opposing Viewpoints is also significantly different from Opposing Viewpoints. As the series title implies, its presentation will help introduce students to the concept of opposing viewpoint, and learn to use this material to aid in critical writing and debate. The series' four-color, accessible format makes the books attractive and inviting to readers of all levels. In addition, each viewpoint has been carefully edited to maximize a reader's understanding of the content. Short but thorough viewpoints capture the essence of an argument. A substantial, thought-provoking essay question placed at the end of each viewpoint asks the student to further investigate the issues raised in the viewpoint, compare and contrast two authors' arguments, or consider how one might go about forming an opinion on the topic at hand. Each viewpoint contains sidebars that include at-a-glance information and handy statistics. A Facts About section located in the back of the book further supplies students with relevant facts and figures.

Following in the tradition of the Opposing Viewpoints series, Greenhaven Press continues to provide readers with invaluable exposure to the controversial issues that shape our world. As John Stuart Mill once wrote: "The only way in which a human being can make some approach to knowing the whole of a subject is by hearing what can be said about it by persons of every variety of opinion and studying all modes in which it can be looked at by every character of mind. No wise man ever acquired his wisdom in any mode but this." It is to this principle that Introducing Issues with Opposing Viewpoints books are dedicated.

Introduction

The USA PATRIOT Act was born out of the tragedy and terror of the September 11, 2001, attacks . . . a legislative solution to a national, international, political, financial, and security problem. Since its inception it has been a source of deep controversy: While nearly all Americans agree that fighting terrorism must be a major priority for the nation, they sharply disagree on how to best address it. In 2006 these debates were rekindled when the Patriot Act was reauthorized by Congress and the president. Though the Patriot Act has gone through many changes since its beginnings, the questions it raises about liberty, security, and the character of the nation remain as relevant as they were when the act first became law.

When the Patriot Act was reauthorized in 2006, officials were voting mainly on pieces of it known as "sunset" provisions. In 2001 some of the act's provisions were so sensitive that Congress put temporary deadlines on them, deadlines that would sunset, or expire, at the end of 2006. These sensitive provisions gave authorities tools they claimed they needed to catch terrorists, but they also gave Congress and the American public time to test out the provisions to see if they unreasonably threatened freedom and liberty. These sunset provisions included section 209, which gives authorities the power to seize voicemail messages with warrants, and 201, which gives the power to intercept wire, oral, and electronic communications relating to terrorism. The 2006 reauthorization made these and other sunset provisions permanent, which means these individual sections will not be voted on again.

Congress, however, voted to make other sections of the act temporary again. These sections, such as 206, which gives authorities the power to conduct roving surveillance wiretaps, and 215, which gives authorities access to a variety of personal records (the so-called "Library Provision"), are now due to sunset December 31, 2009. As a result of the controversy that has surrounded these two provisions, the 2006 version of the Patriot Act provides for greater congressional and judicial oversight of them and also requires high-level approval to access records that are seizable under them.

The terrorist attacks on September 11, 2001, which included the attacks on the World Trade Center in New York City, prompted the United States government to create the Patriot Act in order to better respond to issues of national and international security.

The reauthorization also added new provisions to the Patriot Act that had not been there before. Like their earlier counterparts, these new provisions heralded another wave of disagreement and debate. One such section is the Combat Methamphetamine Epidemic Act of 2005. This bill makes it more difficult to buy several ingredients used to make methamphetamine, a dangerous, addictive, and illegal drug. According to some, such as Congressman Charlie Dent (a Republican from Pennsylvania), this clause belongs in the Patriot Act because of the relationship drug trafficking has to terrorism, and because of the drug's danger on its own. Said Dent, "The growing availability of methamphetamine is a form of terrorism unto itself."[1] Yet others questioned the relationship of the methamphetamine provision to terrorism, claiming the government was using antiterrorism legislation as an excuse to push through a grab bag of unrelated laws. For example, one piece of the law could reportedly place Americans who buy a certain type of cold medicine on a government watch list; another could possibly be used to enlarge powers that have previously been used to prosecute fishermen who illegally catch immature lobsters. For these reasons, reporter John Berlau is one person who has argued that new parts of the Patriot Act are unrelated to terrorism, claiming that "these vast new police powers . . . serve no purpose in the ongoing and serious struggle against terrorism."[2]

The 2006 reauthorization included several other changes and additions that were of less controversy but still of great importance. Under the new act a position for an assistant attorney general for national security was created, which would allow the Justice Department to bring its intelligence surveillance operations under one authority. The new Patriot Act also expands the list for acceptable wiretap orders to include more than twenty federal crimes. It also made permanent fourteen other sections that were set to expire, including section 203, which gives authorities the power to share criminal investigative information, and section 214, which offers pen register and trap-and-trace authority to officials.

But if certain provisions of the Patriot Act have changed, the basic arguments surrounding their existence have not. The enduring

Wisconsin senator Russell Feingold, who had the only dissenting vote to the first version of the Patriot Act, speaks to the press about his concerns over revisions to the act in 2006.

questions about the effect the Patriot Act has had on American society and what values Americans want to support during this unprecedented time in American history remain on the table and vigorously debated. Some continue to view the act as critical to capturing terrorists before they strike. Indeed, supporters of the Patriot Act stand by the initial assumption that because the September 11 antagonists had so thoroughly blended into American life, authorities would have to inspect even the most seemingly ordinary citizens in order to weed out the terrorists among them. And critics of the Patriot Act continue to regard it as an infringement on individual privacy and a threat to the civil liberties of all Americans. These people argue that portions of the Patriot Act threaten to curb their right to privacy and other liberties under the guise of helping authorities catch terrorists. In this way, the words of Senator Russell Feingold, spoken when he cast the lone dissenting vote against the first version of the Patriot Act, continue to ring true for many Americans: "Preserving our freedom is one of the main reasons that we are now engaged in this new war on terrorism. We will lose that war without firing a shot if we sacrifice the liberties of the American people."[3]

The Patriot Act's past and its future will continue to be a keystone of debate for the American public in the post–September 11 world. To this end, *Introducing Issues with Opposing Viewpoints: The Patriot Act* exposes readers to the basic debates surrounding one of the nation's most controversial pieces of legislation. Chapters explore whether and to what extent the Patriot Act fights terrorism, whether and to what extent it violates civil liberties, and who is most threatened by the provisions in the act. Thought-provoking questions encourage students to form their own opinions on the matter and weigh in on this enduring and fascinating topic.

Notes

1. Quoted in John Berlau, "Making a Meth of the PATRIOT Act," *Reason*, February 23, 2006. www.reason.com/news/show/117336 .html.
2. Berlau, "Making a Meth of the PATRIOT Act."
3. Russell Feingold, address to the U.S. Senate, Washington, D.C., October 25, 2001.

Chapter 1

Does the Patriot Act Fight Terrorism?

Many Americans feel the Patriot Act is not an effective tool against terrorism.

The Patriot Act Is a Good Antiterrorism Tool

Robert J. Caldwell

"The foiled British bomb plot shows exactly why we need a Patriot Act."

In the following viewpoint author Robert J. Caldwell argues that the United States needs antiterrorism laws such as the Patriot Act in order to thwart terrorists. He suggests that terrorists are fanatics motivated by a hatred of Western culture and values. Caldwell calls on Americans to support laws such as the Patriot Act that help authorities disrupt terrorist plots. He explains how strong counterterrorism laws helped British authorities prevent a 2006 plot in which terrorists planned to bring down ten airplanes over the Atlantic Ocean. Because of these laws, British officials were able to gather key information that prevented thousands of people from being killed. Caldwell concludes that the United States needs to adopt a similar approach to fighting terrorism and thus should support the Patriot Act so the American intelligence community can prevent future terrorist plots from being carried out.

Robert J. Caldwell, "British Terror Plot Shows Why U.S. Needs the Patriot Act," *Human Events*, vol. 62, August 21, 2006, p. 16. Copyright © 2006 Human Events Inc. Reproduced by permission.

12   The Patriot Act

Caldwell is editor of the *San Diego Union-Tribune*'s Sunday Insight section of opinion and commentary. He writes frequently on political affairs, national defense, and social policy.

AS YOU READ, CONSIDER THE FOLLOWING QUESTIONS:

1. What nationalities were the two dozen conspirators of the British terror plot, as reported by the author?
2. What makes the author think that poverty and oppression were not motivating factors for the British terrorists?
3. What does the word *jihadists* mean in the context of the viewpoint?

The thwarted British bomb plot reveals, once again, the hideous face of terrorism in the modern world.[1] But for the vigilance of Britain's MI5 internal security service, with vital help from American and Pakistani intelligence agencies, 10 jumbo jets flying from Britain to the United States would likely have been blown out of the sky. The potential death toll—3,000 or so people aboard the planes, plus many more dead on the ground if the aircraft crashed into American cities—would have equaled or surpassed the 9/11 catastrophe.

British Scotland Yard Inspector Paul Stephenson put it aptly enough: "This was intended to be mass murder on an unimaginable scale."

The Terrorist War Against Civilization

What manner of war is this when murderous fanatics plot to slaughter, quite deliberately, thousands of innocents? For any among us who are still in denial, for any still tempted to dismiss the war on terror as political hype, what say you now?

What more evidence would you need after the bombings of our embassies in East Africa, after the Khobar Towers and the U.S.S. *Cole*, after the World Trade Center, after Bali and Madrid, after

1. Airplanes at Heathrow Airport in London were grounded when authorities uncovered a terror plot to blow up trans-Atlantic flights to the United States on August 10, 2006.

Many people argue that the strong counterterrorism laws included in the Patriot Act allow security officials to respond more quickly to terrorist threats.

the London subway bombings, and now this, to conclude the inescapable—that this is a war of sheer barbarism waged-against civilization itself?

Why Do Terrorists Target America?

The two dozen alleged conspirators, bomb makers and would-be suicide killers apprehended in dawn police raids in Britain are described as mostly young British Muslims of Pakistani descent. What might their motives have been?

Poverty and oppression? They lived in the leafy, middle-class suburbs of London, to which their parents and grandparents eagerly emigrated.

The war in Lebanon? Their monstrous plot to blow up civilian airliners in midflight was many months in the making, starting long before the fire in the Levant.

British support for Israel? Britain has been studiously even-handed for half a century in the Arab-Israeli conflict.

Britain's role in Iraq? British troops are concentrated in Basra where they serve mainly to protect a heavily Shiite Muslim population from terrorist attacks.

Britain in Afghanistan? British soldiers there defend a freely elected Muslim government as part of a multinational NATO [North Atlantic Treaty Organization] and American force invited to help preserve Afghanistan's 2001 liberation.

The jihadists' case against America, exemplar of the West and friend of Israel, is more obvious. But remember that al Qaeda's jihadists were killing Americans years before George W. Bush was President and before anyone invaded Iraq. Remember, too, that planning for 9/11 began when Bill Clinton was President.

A "Sick Ideology of Lethal Hatred"

No, this is jihadist rage against all things West—indeed, against all things non-Muslim. From [terrorist Osama] bin Laden's al Qaeda to Hezbollah, Hamas, Islamic jihad and terrorist cells from Hamburg to Herat to Hyderabad to India's Mumbai, the goal is the global Islamic caliphate—conversion by the sword.

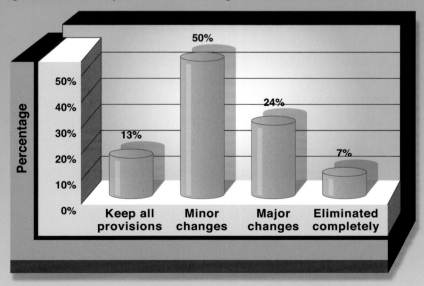

Americans Believe the Patriot Act Is a Good Law

A 2006 poll found that most Americans believe the Patriot Act is a good law that only needs to be changed a little bit, if at all.

Taken from: *USA Today*/CNN Gallup Poll, January 6–8, 2006. www.usatoday.com/news/polls/2006-01-09-poll.htm.

To these deadly zealots, we are all "crusaders and Jews," legitimate targets fit only for Iranian President Mahmoud Ahmadinejad's prescription for Israel: to be "wiped off the map."

Yes, for every jihadist twisting Islam into a creed of violence and terror there are many thousands of Muslims who practice their faith peacefully, are exemplary citizens of countries around the world and who abhor terrorism. But that still leaves legions of radicals willing to stop at nothing in pursuit of their messianic 7th-Century dream of Islamic glory and dominance. For them, we are all targets. For them, the Western world especially is a living affront to Islam.

It is for this sick ideology of lethal hatred and intolerance that dozens of homegrown jihadists in Britain schemed to wreak a bloodbath equaling 9/11.

We Need to Fight the War on Terror with Intelligence

That they failed is a tribute to good intelligence, the front-line soldiery of the war on terror. Reportedly, that intelligence began with an alarm-ringing tip from Pakistan and was vitally amplified by America's Central Intelligence Agency [CIA] and no doubt, by the signals-monitoring National Security Agency [NSA]. The painstaking work in the trenches was done over many months by Britain's MI5, the U.K.'s highly competent internal security service.

Only the determinedly dense could miss the obvious lessons in this for America's own debates over counterterrorism intelligence gathering.

The Patriot Act Can Prevent Terrorist Attacks

A beleaguered President [George W.] Bush could score some useful points by noting that the foiled British bomb plot shows exactly why we need a Patriot Act[2] an NSA free to monitor terrorist communi-

---

2. The Uniting and Strengthening America by Providing Appropriate Tools Required to Intercept and Obstruct Terrorism (USA PATRIOT) Act of 2001.

cations and a Treasury Department–CIA team tracking terrorist finances. What's it worth to prevent another 9/11 and save thousands of lives?

The roots of Britain's parliamentary democracy date back 800 years. That doesn't preclude Britain from wielding MI5 as a bulwark against domestic terrorism without having its secrets printed in the newspapers and its life-saving work hobbled by naive critics living in a dream world. There's a lesson there for Americans who might not want to be blown up on their next trans-Atlantic flight.

So, this time the horror was averted. Let there be no excuse now for not knowing our enemy and not doing what it takes to defend ourselves and our civilization.

EVALUATING THE AUTHOR'S ARGUMENTS:

In this viewpoint Robert J. Caldwell argues that Islamic fanatics plot terrorist attacks not because they are poor, oppressed, or angry about wars in Lebanon, Iraq, or Afghanistan, but because they hate Western civilization. What does Caldwell mean by this, and how is this idea related to supporting laws like the Patriot Act? Use examples from the text to support your answer.

The Patriot Act Is Not a Good Antiterrorism Tool

Julie Hurwitz

"There is nothing in the Patriot Act that would have prevented the events of 9/11."

In the following viewpoint author Julie Hurwitz contends that the United States does not need the Patriot Act to fight terrorism. In Hurwitz's opinion, the United States already had laws to protect it from terrorism: These were passed after the 1993 attack on the World Trade Center. Had authorities used these laws, the September 11, 2001, attacks could have been prevented. Hurwitz argues that this shows the Patriot Act is an unnecessary law, and she asserts that it comes at a great cost to Americans. Among other things, it compromises civil liberties, violates free speech, and threatens the right to protest. For this reason, Hurwitz urges Americans to speak out against the Patriot Act or risk losing their constitutional rights. Hurwitz is a civil rights attorney who lives in Detroit. She is also the executive director of the National Lawyers Guild Maurice and Jane Sugar Law Center for Economic and Social Justice.

Julie Hurwitz, "The PATRIOT Act: Darkness with No Sunset," *Solidarity*, September 2, 2006. www.solidarity-US.org. Reproduced by permission.

AS YOU READ, CONSIDER THE FOLLOWING QUESTIONS:

1. According to the author, which two groups of people have mostly been taken into custody as a result of 9/11?

2. What types of nonterrorism criminal cases have been investigated under the Patriot Act, as reported by the author?

3. What are the "sunset provisions," as described by Hurwitz?

A report by Amnesty International released May 13, 2005 concluded that the treatment of detainees being held around the world, including Guantanamo, in the United States' "war on terror," as glaring and systematic violations of human rights, describing the conditions at the Guantanamo Detention Center as "the gulag of our times, entrenching the notion that people can be detained without any recourse to the law." How did this happen—inside and outside U.S. borders?

A Violation of Basic Rights

On September 11, 2001, we all watched with horror as terrorists targeted the World Trade Center, and thousands of innocent Americans lost their lives. However, what we have seen, allegedly in response to 9/11, has had little or nothing to do with actually fighting terrorism. Since September 2001, literally thousands of people—most, but not all, of them immigrants and people of Arab descent—have been taken into custody in blatant violation of basic constitutional rights.

Citizens and non-citizens alike have been held incommunicado, with no criminal charges brought against them and without even the right to consult with their lawyers; lawyers are being surveilled in their communications with clients, and prosecuted for vigorously defending them, obliterating the protection of the attorney-client privilege.

Repressive Legislation

We are witnessing the passage of more and more repressive legislation, starting in October 2001 with the oxymoronic USA Patriot Act, passed under the extreme pressure of the circumstances in October 2001. The Act itself has less to do with legitimately protecting our security than with waging a war on our fundamental rights under the Constitution. . . .

While supposedly intended to strengthen law enforcement's capacity to prevent another 9/11, there is nothing in the Patriot Act that would have prevented the events of 9/11. On the contrary, its provisions are really a grab bag of governmental powers that had been sought over the years preceding 9/11, and rejected as antithetical to civil liberties.

History has taught us that repressive laws adopted in previous times of crisis (like the Alien and Sedition Act of 1798; restrictions on free speech, and the notorious "Palmer Raids" during WWI; the internment of Japanese-Americans during WWII; blacklists and domestic spying during and after the Cold War/McCarthy era) were eventually recognized as unnecessary at best, and dangerous.

Sufficient Legislation Already Exists

In fact, U.S. law enforcement agencies already possessed more than adequate powers to address the threats at hand long before September 2001. This point has received far too little attention: The FBI [Federal Bureau of Investigation] is on record as stating that the 1993 anti-terrorism legislation (passed in the wake of the first bombing attack on the World Trade Center) provided the agency with sufficient "valuable tools [to be] the keystone to a successful operation" against sophisticated foreign terrorists. We now know that before September 11, the government already had voluminous information in its possession, both about the likelihood of major attacks to come in the near future and even about several of the 9/11 terrorists themselves, but had not bothered to read, review, analyze or act upon that information. With this as the backdrop, it is self-evident that rather than enact new and more repressive laws, the government instead should be devoting its resources to better train its officers and to better enforce and implement the laws already on the books. . . .

Despite many claims that the Patriot Act is specifically intended to fight the "war against terrorism," there are numerous situations where the Act was invoked in "garden variety" criminal cases having nothing to do with terrorism investigations. Thus the Act has been used in the following criminal investigations: seizure of a con man's assets;

In his 2004 State of the Union address, President George W. Bush defended the Patriot Act, stating that it was an "essential tool" in fighting terrorism. Many, however, argue that the act is unnecessary and infringes on constitutional rights.

drug dealer investigations; computer hackers; money launderers. In May 2002, a federal law enforcement bulletin was circulated to U.S. attorneys around the country with regard to the Patriot Act, which stated: "Indeed, investigations of all manner of criminal conduct with nexus to Internet have benefited from these amendments."

The Patriot Act Should Not Be Renewed

The "Son of Patriot I"[1] could be worse than the Son of a Bush. In his January 2004 State of the Union address, President George W.

[1] That is, a second version of the Patriot Act, known as Patriot II, which was passed into law in 2006.

Bush broadly endorsed the Act, saying that it is an "essential tool," and that ". . . the terrorist threat will not expire [when the Patriot Act does]."

There continue to be active attempts by the Bush administration and Congressional Republicans to make the Act and its inroads on our rights and liberties permanent. In May 2004, ten Republican senators introduced a bill designed to eliminate the sunset provisions included in the original Act. One sponsor, Sen. Jon Kyl (R-AZ), noted that he would welcome the Patriot Act provisions "into the foreseeable future." Although many of the most abusive provisions of the Patriot Act were originally slated to be in effect for only five years, scheduled to expire as "sunset provisions" on December 31, 2005, the Bush regime has called for the complete renewal of the Act.

Increased Government Authority

Substantially expanding the legal definition of "terrorist" to include unknowing association with suspected terrorist groups and unknowing support of designated terrorist groups, the proposed "Domestic Security Enhancement Act" (aka "Patriot II," secretly prepared by Justice Department officials shortly before the invasion of Iraq) would authorize the government to strip any American of his or her citizenship who, knowingly or unknowingly, supports a suspected terrorist organization.

> **FAST FACT**
>
> According to the U.S. Department of State, there were 355 international terrorist attacks in 2001. By 2005, there were 11,111 incidents of international terrorism.

An innocent donation to an overseas orphanage that the Justice Department or the Bush administration claims is associated with a suspected terrorist organization could result in the unprecedented loss of citizenship! (Notably, Nelson Mandela's African National Congress would have, for much of its existence, been defined as a terrorist organization under the Patriot Act.) It would even further decrease judicial review, and create fifteen new death penalty crimes, including "domestic terrorism:" If an antiwar protester broke the law during a demonstration, and someone died at that demonstration, the individual could be executed and the organizers charged with domestic terrorism. It would further limit public access to information, even previously public information under the Clean Air Act and other environmental protection laws. To this day, Senate Republicans and the Bush administration are actively pursuing the extension and expansion of the Act, seeking, among other things, to permanently expand the FBI's surveillance and investigative powers to issue administrative subpoenas. This would give the FBI blanket authority to subpoena records from anyone alleged by them to be relevant to a "terrorism investigation," without being required to present any facts to corroborate the claim or even to get a judge's rubber stamp approval. As recently as May 27, 2005, the Bush administration continues to use the same rhetoric, saying that such an expansion of law enforcement power "provides the FBI with essential tools in fighting terrorism."

Increased Domestic Surveillance

The proposed expanded version of the Patriot Act would give the government even more sweeping powers to increase domestic surveillance, solely in the discretion of the executive branch, and without judicial review. It would authorize massive surveillance of individuals and groups who are engaged in lawful, protected protest and free speech activities; terminate all state court consent decrees that limit police agencies from gathering information about individuals and organizations, basic civil liberties protections that had been won in a long series of "red squad" cases; allow even broader warrantless searches of libraries and bookstores; authorize warrantless wiretaps for up to fifteen days, at the sole discretion of the attorney general; and authorize secret arrests. . . .

Be Afraid of the Patriot Act

Now is the time to renew our demands and build on our successes. Several organizations around the country are doing significant work to challenge the assault on fundamental constitutional rights, including the National Lawyers Guild, the Center for Constitutional Rights, the ACLU [American Civil Liberties Union] and the Bill of Rights Defense Committee. We must continue to speak out, dissent and insist on preserving our rights to protest and organize. Use those rights, or lose them.

Be afraid. Be very afraid. But be more afraid of what will happen if we do not speak, if we do not resist, if we do not fight back! We have much more to fear by our silence than by our dissent.

> **EVALUATING THE AUTHOR'S ARGUMENTS:**
>
> Julie Hurwitz ends her viewpoint by warning the reader to speak out against the Patriot Act or lose the right to protest. Do you agree with her warning, or would you characterize her warning as a scare tactic? Explain your answer.

The United States Needs the Patriot Act to Fight Terror

Edward I. Koch

"The Patriot Act, imperfect as it may be, . . . , [is]urgently needed in this war against civilized society."

In the following viewpoint author Edward I. Koch argues that because terrorists kill innocent civilians, it is important for the police force to be given all the tools that would help them effectively fight the war on terror. In the author's opinion, this includes the Patriot Act. Koch says the Patriot Act would create laws that would allow police to prevent death from terrorist attacks, enabling them to carry weapons; to shoot potential terrorists with the intention of killing them; and to receive the support of the public, especially when mistakes are accidentally made. The author believes that public criticism undermines police efforts to catch terrorists, and thus the public should tolerate occasional mistakes that are made in the name of fighting terror. Koch concludes that the Patriot Act is needed to support police and help prevent terrorist attacks against Western civilization.

Edward I. Koch, "The Patriot Act Is Necessary in the Fight Against Terrorism," Newsmax.com, July 27, 2005. Reproduced by permission of the author.

Edward I. Koch is an author, lawyer, and talk radio host. He was a member of the U.S. Congress and, for twelve years, the mayor of New York City.

AS YOU READ, CONSIDER THE FOLLOWING QUESTIONS:

1. According to the author, how many members of Congress voted in favor of reauthorizing the Patriot Act?
2. Who is Ken Livingstone, as described by the author?
3. Describe how the police force is affected by public criticism and lack of support, in Koch's opinion.

"The choice is not between order and liberty. It is between liberty with order and anarchy without either. There is a danger that, if the court does not temper its doctrinaire logic with a little practical wisdom, it will convert the constitutional Bill of Rights into a suicide pact."

That is what Justice Robert H. Jackson said in his dissent in a free-speech case in 1949 when, according to Internet encyclopedia Wikipedia, "the majority opinion, by Justice William O. Douglas, overturned the disorderly conduct conviction of a priest whose anti-Semitic, pro-Nazi rantings at a rally had incited a riot. The court held that Chicago's breach-of-the-peace ordinance violated the First Amendment."

Terrorists Do Not Play by the Rules

Yet in Congress [in July 2005], when the Patriot Act, dealing with a far greater danger to this country, was reauthorized by a vote of 257 to 171, 17 members of the House of Representatives from New York voted against it. They are: Ackerman, Bishop, Crowley, Engel, Hinchey, Israel, Lowey, Maloney, McCarthy, McNulty, Meeks, Nadler, Owens, Serrano, Towns, Velazquez and Weiner, all Democrats.

[In July 2005] in London, an innocent man, by admission of the London police, was shot to death by a police officer and, according to *The New York Times*, that has "revived and fueled an already tense debate over the arming of British police officers." Most London po-

As a proponent of the Patriot Act, former New York mayor Ed Koch, believes that the laws supported by the act are necessary to aid police in their efforts to prevent and fight terrorism.

lice officers are unarmed. Most of the English underworld has apparently responded by not carrying guns themselves.

Terrorists don't play by the same rules. They have no respect for Western laws or traditions. They carry explosives and are prepared to and have, in fact, blown themselves up in a number of incidents worldwide, killing on occasion, when stopped by a security officer, themselves and the officer.

The London bombings on 7/7[1] are the first introduction of the use of suicide bombers in Europe. By stopping a terrorist, the officer may

[1] Four Islamist suicide bombers hit London's public transport system with a series of bomb blasts during the morning rush hour on July 7, 2005.

be preventing many more deaths of innocent civilians while risking his own life. Should reasonable and responsible people deny British police officers assigned to the task of preventing terrorism the permission they have been given to bear arms?

About 10 percent of the London police force, about 2,000 officers, fall into this category. In the case of the shooting of the innocent man, a Brazilian, the London police have, according to *The Times*, "started a formal inquiry." What has been made public before the inquiry reported in *The Times* is the following:

On the Defensive

"The police had believed the man, who was shot at 10 a.m. Friday at the Stockwell subway station in south London, was a would-be suicide bomber because he had left an apartment under surveillance. They said the man behaved in a 'highly suspicious' manner—he was wearing a winter coat on a warm summer day, repeatedly ignored officers' instructions to stop and jumped over the subway turnstiles before running toward a waiting train and tripping and falling to its floor, the police said. Stunned witnesses said a police officer used a pistol to shoot the man five times, at point-blank range, in the head."

> ### FAST FACT
>
> President Bush has said the USA PATRIOT Act helped law enforcement break up terror cells in Ohio, New York, Oregon, and Virginia and prosecute terrorist operatives and supporters in California, Texas, New Jersey, Illinois, Washington, and North Carolina.

Why did what appears to be an execution take place and is now defended by the London Metropolitan police? Ken Livingstone, mayor of London, is accused by some in Britain of being supportive of the aims of terrorists elsewhere in the world, defined as seeking to achieve their political goals through tactics which include the deliberate killing of innocent civilians. Red Ken, which is how he is known in Britain, apparently sees such people on occasion as militants or freedom fighters, in effect excusing their tactics, if the terror is visited on Israeli civilians, including children, women and men.

Contents of the Patriot Act

The Patriot Act is broken down into ten titles that each deal with a different aspect of law enforcement and security.

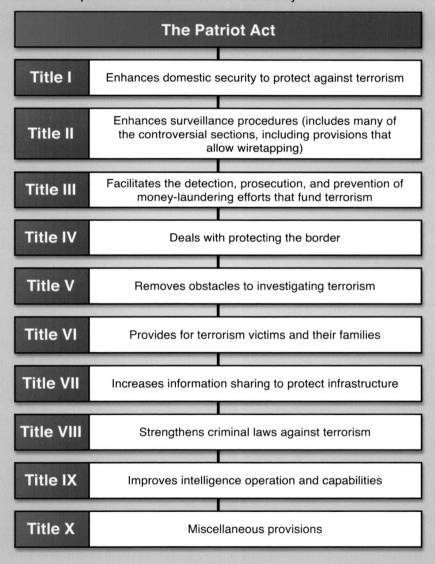

The Patriot Act	
Title I	Enhances domestic security to protect against terrorism
Title II	Enhances surveillance procedures (includes many of the controversial sections, including provisions that allow wiretapping)
Title III	Facilitates the detection, prosecution, and prevention of money-laundering efforts that fund terrorism
Title IV	Deals with protecting the border
Title V	Removes obstacles to investigating terrorism
Title VI	Provides for terrorism victims and their families
Title VII	Increases information sharing to protect infrastructure
Title VIII	Strengthens criminal laws against terrorism
Title IX	Improves intelligence operation and capabilities
Title X	Miscellaneous provisions

Compiled by editor.

Livingstone, faced with continuing terror tactics against the city he leads, explained the new British police policy that now includes shoot-to-kill orders in some circumstances, is quoted in *The Times* as saying, "If you are dealing with someone who might be a suicide bomber, if they remain conscious they could trigger plastic explosives or whatever device is on them. And therefore overwhelmingly in these circumstances, it is going to be a shoot-to-kill policy."

The Times further reports, "Police guidelines for dealing with suspected suicide bombers recommend shooting at the head rather than the body in case the suspect is carrying explosives."

That policy makes common sense to me.

Avoiding a Premature, Rushed Report

There will be an official inquiry in London. That report will undoubtedly be made public. Whether it bears out the facts as alleged by the London Police Department, only time will tell. When I was mayor and with Police Commissioner Ben Ward attended crime scenes throughout the city, I knew, having been told by Ward, that on many occasions the alleged facts initially reported by the police to the press would turn out to be inaccurate in some respects. Ward explained that the presence of the press and demands for information, and even my presence, could cause a premature, rushed public report that upon further analysis would show errors in the first released statement.

We know that happened in London after the 7/7 bombings. *The Times*, discussing this aspect of the case, reported, "However, in this enormously important inquiry, Scotland Yard has often rushed to release relevant developments. But the result has been the risk of divulging incomplete or even wrong information to a demanding public . . . the police have made a number of high-profile public statements that they were later forced to retract or modify."

Let the Police Do Their Job

We here in the U.S. and those on the ground should, under these circumstances, hold our own lethal fire, in this case, criticism of the police, until the official inquiry has been concluded. Public criticism of the police force without knowing all the facts can promote fear in the police force and a belief that they are viewed as villains instead of protectors.

We depend, in London, New York City and everywhere else, on our police forces to protect us, often at great personal risk to themselves. If they see a lack of public support and therefore lose confidence in themselves, and decide that doing as little as possible in their response is their best defense, we the public will suffer.

Why We Need the Patriot Act

Let us remember Justice Jackson's words and their relevance to the war against terrorism. Democracies, when attacked as we have been by Islamic fanatics, must examine what they must do to prevail against the enemy. That cannot be limited simply to the size and quality of the personnel and the arms they bear. It also requires that we create appropriate laws needed to protect us, some of which will be far more intrusive than we would accept in peacetime; and provide law enforcement with constitutional and critically needed statutes that will permit them to apprehend and convict criminals engaged in terrorism who threaten not only individuals, but all of Western civilization.

The Patriot Act, imperfect as it may be, now renewed by the House and awaiting Senate action, is urgently needed in this war against civilized society.

EVALUATING THE AUTHOR'S ARGUMENTS:

The author chose to open his viewpoint with a quote from Justice Robert H Jackson. How does the quote relate to the author's main argument? Did you find this to be an effective way to capture a reader's attention? Explain why or why not.

The United States Does Not Need the Patriot Act to Fight Terror

Bob Barr

> "*The USA Patriot Act is a legislative grab bag that does little to encourage better law enforcement and intelligence work.*"

Bob Barr represented Georgia in the U.S. House of Representatives from 1995 to 2003. In the following viewpoint he argues that the Patriot Act does not provide law enforcement personnel with any useful terror fighting tools. He suggests that the laws that existed prior to the Patriot Act were strong enough to fight terrorists —the problem is that they were not properly enforced. He accuses lawmakers of using the Patriot Act as an excuse to pass sweeping and threatening laws that had previously been denied to them. Barr states that Americans do not need more antiterrorism laws—they simply need better enforcement of laws that are already on the books. For this reason, he concludes that the Patriot Act does not offer Americans any extra protection from terrorism.

AS YOU READ, CONSIDER THE FOLLOWING QUESTIONS:

1. What pre–Patriot Act laws did the September 11, 2001, terrorists break, according to Barr?

2. What happened as a result of Congress not wanting to look soft on terrorism, in Barr's opinion?

3. What excuse did the September 11 attacks provide lawmakers with, according to Barr?

T
he USA Patriot Act of 2001 and the proposed Son of Patriot Act,[1] [is] now [2003] debated in the Congress at the request of the Bush administration.

These are frightening laws. Left unchecked, they threaten the constitutional basis on which our society is premised: that citizens possess rights over their persons and property and that they retain those rights unless there is a sound, articulated, and specific reason for the government to take them away (i.e., probable cause of criminal activity). The Fourth Amendment's guarantee against unreasonable search and seizure will have been gutted.

We Already Had Laws to Prevent Terrorism

Possibly the measures contained in the Patriot Act, its proposed new offspring, and numerous other official surveillance measures now in effect or being planned were, as we're told, essential responses to the terrorist attacks of September 11, 2001. Possibly they are specifically tailored to meet such threats in the future, and the best and most efficient way to minimize the likelihood of such attacks. Perhaps then one could accept some of the encroachments on civil liberties as necessary and perhaps even worthwhile. But they're not.

The terrorists who gained access to those four jetliners in the early morning of September 11, 2001, carried weapons that were already illegal on commercial aircraft. They were already in this country illegally, or had overstayed their lawful presence. Their pockets were stuffed with false identification. Their knowledge of the aircraft's performance and handling had been gathered in violation of federal law.

[1] That is, expanded Patriot Act laws that were passed in 2006.

Bob Barr, former Georgia congressman, argues that the laws that existed before the Patriot Act were sufficient for fighting terrorism.

Much of the information that could have alerted law enforcement officials to their horrendous plot was already within the possession of law enforcement and intelligence agencies. The government had sufficient lawful power to identify and stop the plotters. It failed to do so.

Yet what was the response to this tragedy? Did a single federal agency or official come before the American people and say: "We're sorry. We had the power to stop these terrorists. We had sufficient money to have done so. We simply made mistakes and errors in judgment, which will now be corrected." Not a chance.

A Chance to Increase Government Power

Instead, what we saw—and I saw personally, as a member of both the House Judiciary Committee and the Government Reform Committee —was agency after agency, bureaucrat after bureaucrat come before

© 2005 Andy Singer and PoliticalCartoons.com.

us and say, "You [the Congress] didn't give us enough legal power or money to stop these attacks. We need more money. We need more power." But not wishing to appear soft on terrorism, the Congress—not surprisingly—gave them very nearly whatever they asked for.

And what they asked for definitely was not narrowly tailored, limited, or designed only to correct those specific provisions of existing laws that needed to be tweaked. What the bureaucrats sought—and largely got—were far-reaching powers that applied not just to antiterrorism needs but to virtually *all* federal criminal laws. Challenges to wiretapping laws, to search and seizures, easier access to tangible evidence—the list is long and complex. In essence, the attacks of September 11 provided an excuse for the executive branch to pull off the shelf, dust off, and push into law a whole series of proposals it had sought unsuccessfully for years.

Moreover, the direction Washington is now turning—making it easier to gather evidence on *everyone* within our borders, in an effort to develop profiles of terrorists and identify them amid the masses of data—is not likely to be particularly successful at thwarting terrorist attacks. As the CIA itself noted in a unclassified study reportedly conducted in 2001, terrorists typically take great pains to avoid being profiled: they don't want to get caught, and in fact it is essentially impossible to profile terrorists.

We Need Better Law Enforcement, Not More Laws

The real way to catch terrorists is with better intelligence gathering, better coordination and analysis, better utilization of existing law enforcement tools, and quicker and more appropriate dissemination of that intelligence. The key word is *better*. With a few notable exceptions, the USA Patriot Act is a legislative grab bag that does little to encourage *better* law enforcement and intelligence work. Instead, we have an unprecedented expansion of federal law enforcement powers that significantly diminishes the civil liberties of American citizens, with only marginal increases in real security.

These fears are not, as some are saying, unfounded. And all I've done is scratch the surface of what is shaping up as a dramatic alteration to the very foundation of our society. The original Winston Smith [the character from George Orwell's novel *1984*] was scared to death of the power of government—so we should be too. It was Benjamin Franklin, not George Orwell, who said, "They that give up essential liberty to obtain a little temporary safety deserve neither liberty nor safety." But, it could just as well have been.

EVALUATING THE AUTHOR'S ARGUMENTS:

Bob Barr is a former representative who served on the Judiciary Committee and the Government Reform Committee, two groups tasked with making the country's laws, including the Patriot Act. Does knowing Barr's background as a government official influence your opinion of his argument? If so, in what way?

Chapter 2

Does the Patriot Act Violate Civil Liberties?

Demonstrators gather in New York City to protest the Patriot Act. Many Americans believe the act infringes on civil liberties.

The Patriot Act Violates Civil Liberties

Chuck Baldwin

"Instead of helping to win the war on terrorism, the Patriot Act is helping to dismantle fundamental liberties protected by the U.S. Constitution."

In the following viewpoint author Chuck Baldwin argues that federal authorities use the Patriot Act to abuse their powers and take liberties away from the American people in the name of fighting terrorism. Baldwin accuses the Justice Department of grossly overstating the number of terrorism-related crimes that were prosecuted under the Patriot Act: The majority of the convictions were actually for minor, nonterrorism-related crimes, he asserts. Furthermore, police used their new authority to abuse and harass by conducting invasive investigations and using unconstitutional surveillance tactics. The author warns that the Patriot Act will continue to give unregulated and threatening power to future White House administrations. Baldwin concludes by urging Americans not to trade their constitutional liberties for the false promise of security.

Baldwin is the founder and pastor of Crossroads Baptist Church in Pensacola,

Chuck Baldwin, "Patriot Act Is Helping Dismantle Constitutional Liberties," *Chuck Baldwin Live*, June 14, 2005. www.chuckbaldwinlive.com. Reproduced by permission of the author.

Florida. He has written two books on theology and hosts the daily radio call-in show *Chuck Baldwin Live.*

AS YOU READ, CONSIDER THE FOLLOWING QUESTIONS:
1. How many actual convictions for terrorist-related crimes have been made under the Patriot Act, as reported by Baldwin?
2. According to the author, why did America's Founding Fathers place the Bill of Rights into the Constitution?
3. Who is Brandon Mayfield, and how does he figure into the author's argument?

The White House has summoned its Justice Department officials to put on a full court press toward the purpose of convincing Congress to reauthorize portions of the Patriot Act that are scheduled to sunset [expire]. The argument is that the Patriot Act must be renewed in order to help win the war on terrorism. However, instead of helping to win the war on terrorism, the Patriot Act is helping to dismantle fundamental liberties protected by the U.S. Constitution.

The Federal Government Abuses Its Power

The first argument used by the feds is the Justice Department's report that the Patriot Act has been used by law enforcement to conduct investigations leading to the conviction of more than 200 defendants for terrorist-related crimes. However, according to *The Washington Post,* "the numbers are misleading at best."

The Post report of June 12, 2005 stated, "An analysis of the Justice Department's own list of terrorism prosecutions by *The Washington Post* shows that 39 people, not 200, as officials have implied, were convicted of crimes related to terrorism or national security." *The Post* report said, "Most of the others were convicted of relatively minor crimes such as making false statements and violating immigration law and had nothing to do with terrorism."

Would the feds exaggerate and deceive Congress and the American people in order to gain more power? They obviously would and have!

And, unfortunately, it appears that Congress is more than willing to give the White House what it wants.

The Patriot Act Abridges Constitutional Rights

Just recently the Senate Intelligence Committee voted to expand the powers of the FBI "to subpoena records without the approval of a judge or grand jury in terrorism investigations under Patriot Act revisions approved Tuesday [June 7, 2005]." It is the Patriot Act's expansion of federal police power that should be of concern to every freedom-loving citizen in this country!

America's Founding Fathers placed the Bill of Rights into our Constitution to insure that the rights of liberties of our citizens would not be abridged by the insatiable desire of the federal government for

Former United States attorney general Alberto Gonzales appears before a Senate Judiciary Committee hearing on the oversight of the U.S. Department of Justice in 2007. Gonzales and the Department of Justice were criticized for abusing the provisions of the Patriot Act.

limitless power. The Patriot Act is a modern day justification of the founders' wisdom, because abridging liberty is exactly what it does.

Specifically, the Patriot Act eviscerates the Fourth, Fifth, and Sixth Amendments and does serious injury to others. Under Patriot Act provisions, American citizens may be arrested (or even held without being arrested) and incarcerated without being charged with a crime or even without a judge's order. The government does not have to tell the press who has been arrested or where they are being detained.

The Patriot Act Lets Federal Police Abuse Their Authority

The Patriot Act authorizes federal police to perform searches and seizures of private property without warrant. It authorizes federal wiretaps without judicial oversight. It allows the feds to monitor our internet usage, intercept e-mails and internet communications, all without judicial oversight.

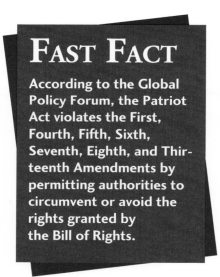

FAST FACT

According to the Global Policy Forum, the Patriot Act violates the First, Fourth, Fifth, Sixth, Seventh, Eighth, and Thirteenth Amendments by permitting authorities to circumvent or avoid the rights granted by the Bill of Rights.

Furthermore, the definitions contained within the Patriot Act of what constitutes "terrorism" is downright Orwellian[1]. For example, according to Congressman Ron Paul (R-TX), "The bill as written defines terrorism as acts intended 'to influence the policy of a government by intimidation or coercion.' Under this broad definition, a scuffle at an otherwise peaceful pro-life demonstration might subject attendees to a federal investigation. We have seen abuses of law enforcement authority in the past to harass individuals or organizations with unpopular political views."

The number of Americans who have been subjected to various kinds of federal investigation and abuse is incalculable. I can tell my readers that I have been victimized by the Department of Homeland Security

---

1. British author George Orwell's description of a situation, idea, or societal condition antithetical to free society, such as an invasion of personal privacy or state control over citizens' daily life.

© 2005 John Trever, *The Albuquerque Journal*, and PoliticalCartoons.com.

when my name appeared on one of its "potential terrorist lists" when I tried to board a Continental flight out of San Antonio, Texas.

According to press reports, thousands of innocent Americans have been subjected to the scrutiny of myriad federal police agencies. It now appears that our federal government has determined that we are guilty until proven innocent. This is not the America that our fathers fought and died to bequeath to us!

The War on Terror Never Ends

Beyond that, as with the federal government's "war on drugs," so too its "war on terrorism" is everlasting. It never ends. Those who suggest that there will be a cessation to the "war on terror" are living in a dream world. Once having established the federal machinery to fight this broad and undefined war, there is no turning back. There can never be a declaration of victory or let up of intensity. The machinery can only become larger and larger.

The line we constantly hear from the Bush administration is, "Trust us. We would never abuse our new found power." Oh, really? Just recently [April 5, 2005] Attorney General Alberto Gonzales admitted that the FBI misused powers contained in the Patriot Act when it searched the home and seized the property of Brandon Mayfield, then used the information to wrongly portray the man as a Muslim militant. How many other federal abuses of power have we not been told about?

However, even if the current Justice Department would not intentionally abuse the provisions of the Patriot Act, what guarantees do the American people have that future departments would be as benign? For example, I wonder how comfortable conservatives would be with the knowledge that President Hillary Clinton's Justice Department had the latitudes and laxities of the Patriot Act at its disposal? Remember, folks, the powers granted to the federal government by the Patriot Act will be enjoyed not only by this administration, but by every administration yet to come!

Do Not Exchange Liberty for Temporary Security

The idea that we must fight terrorism by dismantling the constitutional liberties of the American people is fraught with fallacy! America has fought a revolutionary war, two world wars, and numerous conflicts and, until now, has mostly held the Bill of Rights to be sacred and irrevocable. Suddenly, it asks its citizens to relinquish their liberties in the name of security.

Before the American people surrender their liberties to an ever burgeoning and meddlesome federal bureaucracy, however, we should well remember the sage counsel of Benjamin Franklin who said, "They that give up essential liberty for temporary security deserve neither."

EVALUATING THE AUTHOR'S ARGUMENTS:

To make his argument that the Patriot Act violates civil liberties, Chuck Baldwin describes a personal experience in which his own rights were violated. Describe Baldwin's experience. What happened to him? Did the inclusion of this personal detail make you more likely to agree with his perspective? Why or why not?

The Patriot Act Fights Terrorism While Protecting Civil Liberties

James Jay Carafano and Paul Rosenzweig

"The obligation of the government is a dual one: to protect civil safety and security against violence and to preserve civil liberty."

In the following viewpoint authors James Jay Carafano and Paul Rosenzweig contend that the Patriot Act preserves security while protecting civil liberties. They explain that the Patriot Act was needed to replace old laws that discouraged information sharing between law enforcement and intelligence agencies. To illustrate how barriers were erected under the old laws, Carafano and Rosenzweig cite the case of the 1993 World Trade Center bombing criminal prosecutions, during which the Department of Justice instructed the FBI to separate counterintelligence investigations from criminal prosecutions. The authors suggest this incident contributed to

James Jay Carafano and Paul Rosenzweig, "After the Patriot Act," *Winning the Long War: Lessons from the Cold War for Defeating Terrorism and Preserving Freedom.* Bowie, MD: Heritage Books, Washington, D.C., 2005. Copyright © 2005 by The Heritage Foundation. All rights reserved. Reproduced by permission.

the failure of authorities in preventing the 9/11 attacks. The authors reject the idea that government agencies abuse powers under the Patriot Act and conclude that it safeguards the constitutional rights of Americans while allowing appropriate foreign intelligence information sharing between federal agencies.

Carafano and Rosenzweig are senior research fellows at the Heritage Foundation, a think tank dedicated to promoting conservative public policies.

AS YOU READ, CONSIDER THE FOLLOWING QUESTIONS:

1. What is the "primary purpose" standard, and how did it prevent information sharing between government agencies, in the authors' opinion?
2. What is important about Section 203 and 218 of the Patriot Act, according Carafano and Rosenzweig?
3. Who is Viet Dinh, and what is his opinion of the Patriot Act?

"Business as usual" will not stop twenty-first century terrorism. We need to do things differently. The first step that needs to be taken is to move forward on the successful initiatives that have already been undertaken.

A Wall of Policies Prevented Information Sharing

During the well-publicized hearings of the 9/11 Commission, present and former government officials from both the Clinton and Bush Administrations, Republicans and Democrats, acknowledged that prior to 9/11 a "wall" of legal and regulatory policies prevented effective sharing of information between the intelligence and law enforcement communities. Attorney General John Ashcroft noted that in 1995 the Justice Department embraced legal reasoning that effectively excluded prosecutors from intelligence investigations. At times, for prudential reasons, Justice Department officials even raised the "wall" *higher* than was required by law, to avoid any appearance of "impermissibly" mixing law enforcement and intelligence activities.

Indeed, a very real wall existed. It was based on a standard that allowed the use of intelligence-gathering mechanisms only when foreign intelligence was the "primary purpose" of the activity. This old "primary purpose" standard derived from a series of court decisions. The standard was formally established in written Department of Justice guidelines in July 1995. Although information could be "thrown over the wall" from intelligence officials to prosecutors, the decision to do so always rested with national security personnel—even though law enforcement agents are in a better position to mine what evidence is pertinent to their cases.

Old Rules Allowed Terrorists to Attack

The old legal rules discouraged coordination and created what the Foreign Intelligence Surveillance Court of Review calls "perverse organizational incentives." The wall had some very negative real-world consequences. Former Department of Justice official Victoria Toensing tells of one: In the 1980s [June 1985], terrorists hijacked an airplane, TWA Flight 847, which eventually landed in Lebanon. At the time that negotiations were ongoing, the FBI had the capacity to intercept communications between the hijackers on the plane and certain individuals in America. Negotiations did not, however, advance quickly enough and the terrorists killed an American, Robert Stethem, and dumped his body

onto the airport tarmac on live TV. As a result, the Department of Justice announced its intention to capture and prosecute those responsible, which had the immediate effect of making the FBI's ongoing intercepts no longer for the "primary" purpose of foreign intelligence gathering: The "primary" purpose was now clearly prosecution. As a result, in the middle of a terrorist crisis, the FBI turned *off* its listening devices for fear of violating the rule against

The 1993 bombing of the World Trade Center and the subsequent investigation revealed a culture of information restriction among U.S. intelligence agencies.

using intelligence-gathering techniques in a situation in which intelligence gathering was not the main purpose. It is difficult to conceive of a more wrongheaded course of conduct, yet the FBI, rightly, felt that it was legally required to act as it did.

The Patriot Act Has Proved Its Worth

Nor is this the only instance which the artificial "wall" has deterred vital information sharing between the law enforcement and intelligence communities. Who can forget the testimony of FBI agent Coleen Rowley, who pointed to these very limitations as part of the reason the FBI was not able to "connect the dots" before 9/11. Instead, the culture against information sharing was so deeply ingrained that during the criminal prosecutions for the 1993 World Trade Center bombing, the Department of Justice actually raised the height of the artificial wall. Imposing requirements that went "beyond what is legally required," the Department instructed its FBI agents to "clearly separate" ongoing counterintelligence investigations from the criminal prosecution. There is even some possibility that this wall may have been the contributing factor to our failure to prevent the 9/11 attacks.

Largely in response to these problems, Congress passed the USA Patriot Act subsequent to the September 11 attacks. As Viet Dinh (one of the act's principal authors) concluded, the law "makes the best use of the information we have, sharing information between law enforcement agencies to put the pieces of the puzzle together so we can look for the needle in the haystack." Not only was the legislation needed, it has proved its worth in practice. The law has facilitated dozens of reported terrorist investigations by removing both real and imagined barriers that kept the people trying to protect us from working together. To date, as the Department of Justice Inspector General has reported, there has not been one single instance of abuse of the powers granted in the act.

The Patriot Act Preserves Security and Safeguards Civil Liberties

Safeguarding the civil liberties of American citizens is vitally important, as important during war as during periods of peace. Yet so, too, is preserving our security. The Patriot Act preserves both. Hysterical criticisms that the act was unnecessary and is a threat to a healthy civil society have proven unfounded, and calls for repeal or significant revision are misguided.

Thus, we reject the broadest criticisms of the Patriot Act: that it was unnecessary, that it has added nothing to the efforts to avoid additional terrorist activities, and that it is little more than a "wish list" of law enforcement powers.

In particular, one aspect of the Patriot Act, embodied in Sections 203 and 218, was absolutely vital. Section 203 permits law enforcement information gathered through a grand jury investigation to be shared with intelligence agencies. Section 218 allows the use of intelligence information-gathering mechanisms whenever intelligence gathering is a "significant" purpose of an investigation—and it allows the information gathered to be shared with law enforcement. Taken together, these two sections effectively tear down the "wall" that existed between law enforcement and intelligence agencies and permit inter-agency cooperation.

Enhanced Information Sharing Reduces Terrorist Threats

Sections 203 and 218 empower federal agencies to share information on terrorist activity. This is an important, significant, and positive development. One of the principal criticisms made in virtually every review of our pre–September 11 actions is that we failed to "connect the dots." Indeed, as a congressional review panel noted: "Within the Intelligence Community, agencies did not share relevant counterterrorism information, prior to September 11th. This breakdown in communications was the result of a number of factors, including differences in agencies' missions, legal authorities and cultures."

In short, the Patriot Act changes (as a general principle) adopt the rule that *any information lawfully gathered during a foreign or domestic counterintelligence investigation or lawfully gathered during a domestic law enforcement investigation should be capable of being shared with other federal agencies.* The artificial limitations once imposed on such information sharing are the relics of a bygone era and, in light of the changed nature of the terrorist threat, are of substantially diminished value today.

We have already had at least one test case demonstrating the potential utility of enhanced information sharing between intelligence and law enforcement organizations: the indictment of Sami Al-Arian on charges of providing material support to several Palestinian terrorist organizations. The government's case against Al-Arian is apparently based on foreign counterintelligence wiretap intercepts that date back as far as 1993. According to the information in those wiretaps, Al-Arian is charged with having knowingly provided financing to a terrorist organization with the awareness that the funds he provided would be used to commit terrorist acts. That information has been in the possession of our intelligence organizations for at least the past seven years.

It was not until the passage of the Patriot Act and the ruling of the Foreign Intelligence Surveillance Court of Review (in November 2002) that the intelligence community felt it was legally allowed to provide that information to law enforcement officials. Only those changes allowed the government to file the charges pending against Al-Arian. As the Al-Arian case suggests, to the extent that the law removed longstanding statutory barriers to bringing information gathered in

Congressional Votes on the Patriot Act

The Patriot Act was first voted into law in 2001, shortly after the September 11 terrorist attacks. It was renewed by Congress in 2005 (House) and 2006 (Senate). Though more members of Congress voted against the renewal of the Patriot Act than in the days following September 11, it still overwhelmingly passed.

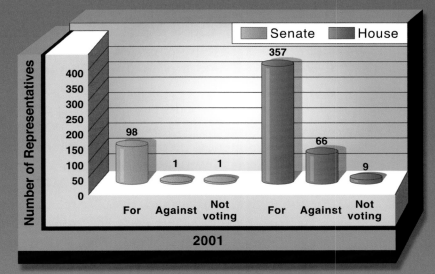

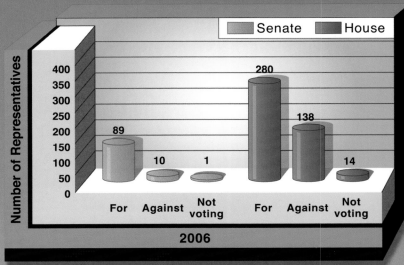

Taken from: U.S. Senate and House of Representatives Roll Call in U.S. Patriot Act 2001 and 2006. www.senate.gov; www.house.gov.

national security investigations into federal criminal courts, it is to be welcomed.

The Right Thing to Do

Nor can it be convincingly argued that these changes violate the Constitution. To the contrary, as the Court of Review made clear, a wall between intelligence and law enforcement is not constitutionally required. The change wrought by the Patriot Act "is a reasonable response based on a balance of the legitimate need of the government for foreign intelligence information to protect against national security threats with the protected rights of citizens." The courts and Congress agree that appropriate information sharing is simply the right thing to do. . . .

The obligation of the government is a dual one: to protect civil safety and security against violence *and* to preserve civil liberty. Viet Dinh used almost the exact same argument to describe the government's role in fighting the war on terrorism: "The function of government is the security of its polity and the safety of its people. For without them there will be no structure so that liberty can survive. We see our work not as a balancing security and liberty," Dinh declared, "rather, we see it as securing liberty by assuring the conditions of true liberty." We can achieve that goal, but there is more work to done.

EVALUATING THE AUTHORS' ARGUMENTS:

In this viewpoint the authors state that the Patriot Act protects civil liberties while successfully fighting the war on terror. What pieces of evidence do the authors provide to support this claim? Did they convince you of their argument? Explain why or why not.

Viewpoint
3

The Patriot Act Violates Americans' Privacy

John W. Whitehead

"If law enforcement officials can search your home and your records without having to go through a judge, then the concept of a man's home being his castle will become as antiquated as the Model T."

In the following viewpoint John W. Whitehead argues that the Patriot Act violates Americans' privacy rights. In Whitehead's opinion, the Patriot Act redefines terrorism in terms that are too broad, allowing authorities to conduct invasive investigations and arrest people for activities that have little to do with terrorism. Furthermore, it gives the government far-reaching powers to access personal records, library records, and Internet sites visited by the person under investigation. In Whitehead's opinion, the most invasive provision of the Patriot Act authorizes a warrantless search, in which the FBI obtains a special warrant to search and seize personal property from a home without having to notify the occupants or go through a judge first. The author concludes that the police force uses extensive powers under the Patriot Act to undermine individuals' basic

John W. Whitehead, "How Liberty Dies: The Patriot Reauthorization Act," The Rutherford Institute, June 13, 2005. Reproduced by permission.

constitutional liberties and move Americans further away from a free nation.

Whitehead is an author and constitutional attorney. He is founder and president of the Rutherford Institute, a nonprofit conservative legal organization.

AS YOU READ, CONSIDER THE FOLLOWING QUESTIONS:

1. According to the author, how many local and county governments have passed legislation that opposes the Patriot Act?
2. Which six amendments does the Patriot Act violate, according to the author?
3. Name at least five ways the author says the Patriot Act allows the government to intrude on the private lives of Americans.

D o our representatives understand how we feel? Or don't they care? The recent approval by the Senate Intelligence Committee to reauthorize and expand the Patriot Act's powers leaves one wondering if Congress listens to the American people anymore. Equally worrisome is the fact that the critical discussions and decisions surrounding expansion of the Act are taking place in secret, behind closed doors. What do our government representatives have to hide?

Many Americans Oppose the Patriot Act

Since the passage of the Patriot Act six weeks after the 9/11 terrorist attacks, 378 local and county governments and seven state legislatures representing millions of Americans have passed resolutions or ordinances opposing aspects of the Patriot Act that they believe to be at odds with the United States Constitution. One City Council member from Arcata, Calif., described his town's ordinance as a nonviolent preemptive attack on the federal government's revision of the Bill of Rights. Yet our government continues to ignore these concerns and push through its own agenda.

At a massive 342 pages, the Patriot Act violates at least six of the ten original amendments known as the Bill of Rights—the First,

Fourth, Fifth, Sixth, Seventh and Eighth Amendments—and possibly the Thirteenth and Fourteenth as well.

The Patriot Act was rushed through Congress, even though the majority of our representatives admitted to not reading it, reassured perhaps by the inclusion of a five-year sunset provision. But that sun does not seem to be setting on this chilling piece of legislation. Instead, the Senate Intelligence Committee is not only working to make the Patriot Act permanent, but also to expand its reach.

The Patriot Act Allows Government Intrusion

Among some of the widely cited concerns about the Patriot Act are that it redefines terrorism so broadly that many non-terrorist political activities such as protest marches or demonstrations and civil disobedience can be considered a terrorist act; grants the FBI the right to come to your place of employment, demand your personal records and question your supervisors and fellow employees, all without notifying you; allows the government access to your medical records, school records and practically every personal record about you; allows the government to secretly demand to see records of books or magazines you've checked out in any public library and Internet sites you've visited (at least 545 libraries re-

FAST FACT

A 126-page audit of the FBI, conducted by the Department of Justice, discovered that agents had obtained citizens' telephone records in nonemergency circumstances and without proper authorization.

ceived such demands in the first year following passage of the Patriot Act); and most egregious of all, it allows the FBI to enter your home through the use of a special warrant, search your personal effects and confiscate your personal property without informing you that they have done so.

Yet despite the many objections to these disturbing provisions within the Patriot Act, the Senate Intelligence Committee has wholeheartedly embraced the Patriot Reauthorization Act (PAREA), which takes government intrusion into the lives of average Americans to a whole new level.

A Direct Assault on the Fourth Amendment

For example, one "administrative authority" provision within PAREA, which would allow the FBI to write and approve its own search orders, represents a direct assault on the Fourth Amendment's prohibitions against unreasonable search and seizure. Yet if Congress acts to approve what critics have termed "carte blanche for a fishing expedition," the FBI will be in a position to conduct warrantless

Much of the opposition to the Patriot Act is centered on its broad definition of terrorism and its far-reaching power to access personal information.

searches on people without having to show any evidence that they may be involved in criminal activities. This provision would also lift one of the last restrictions on special warrants for the FBI, namely, that the information be related to international terrorism or foreign intelligence.

Yet while government officials insist that the FBI needs additional tools to fight terrorism, a recent report suggests that all the FBI really needs to do is its job. A Justice Department report reveals that the same FBI that wants to do an end-run around our Constitution passed up on at least five chances in the months before 9/11 to locate two terrorist hijackers as they prepared for attacks on our country. The oversights were attributed to communication breakdowns, lack of urgency and bureaucratic obstacles, among other things. "What we found were sufficient deficiencies in the way the FBI handled these issues," said Inspector General Glenn Fine. In other words, if the FBI and other intelligence agencies had simply done their jobs and followed up on leads, then there wouldn't have been a need for the Patriot Act and there certainly wouldn't be a need for warrantless searches.

While it remains questionable whether the Patriot Act has really succeeded in protecting Americans against future acts of terrorism, these highly controversial additions to the Act will unquestionably succeed in gutting the Fourth Amendment. Of all the protections found in the Constitution, the Fourth Amendment stands as the final barrier between the privacy rights of Americans and the potential for government abuse of power. But if law enforcement officials can search your home and your records without having to go through a judge, then the concept of a man's home being his castle will become as antiquated as the Model T.

The Patriot Act Undermines Basic Constitutional Rights

Despite the fact that an increasing number of Americans are voicing their concerns about intrusions on their privacy, President Bush continues to express his support for extending the Patriot Act. One day after the 9/11 terrorist attacks, Bush declared, "We will not allow this enemy to win the war by changing our way of life or restricting our freedoms." Yet if Congress succeeds in continuing to pass legislation

Opposition to the United States Patriot Act

As of December 2007, 414 resolutions (including 8 statewide resolutions and several city and county resolutions) have been passed in opposition to the Patriot Act.

States that have passed a statewide resolution:

States that have cities and counties that have passed resolutions:

Arizona
Bisbee
Flagstaff
Jerome
Pima County
Tucson

Arkansas
Eureka Springs

Connecticut
Bethany
Coventry
Hampton
Hartford
Lyme
Mansfield
New Haven
Norwalk
Windham

Delaware
Arden
Odessa
Newark
Wilmington

Florida
Alachua County
Broward County
St. Petersburg
Sarasota
Tampa

Georgia
Atlanta
Savannah

Illinois
Carbondale
Chicago
Evanston
Glencoe
Oak Park

Indiana
Bloomington

Iowa
Ames
Des Moines

Kansas
Kansas City/
Wyandotte County
Lawrence

Kentucky
Lexington-Fayette County

Maryland
Baltimore
Greenbelt
Montgomery County
Prince George's County
Takoma Park

Massachusetts
Acton
Amherst
Aquinnah
Arlington
Ashfield
Brewster
Bridgewater
Brookline
Buckland
Cambridge

Carlisle
Charlemont
Chatham
Chilmark
Colrain
Concord
Conway
Dennis
Duxbury
Eastham
Edgartown
Greenfield
Groton
Heath
Lenox
Leverett
Lexington
Lincoln
Littleton
Lowell
Manchester-by-
the-Sea
Marblehead
Milton
Newton

North Adams
Northampton
Oak Bluffs
Orleans
Peabody
Pittsfield
Provincetown
Rockport
Shutesbury
Somerville
Sudbury
Swampscott
Tisbury
Truro
Wellfleet
Wendell
West Tisbury
Westford
Weston
Williamstown

Michigan
Ann Arbor
Auburn Hills
Detroit
East Lansing
Ferndale
Grand Rapids
Ingham County
Kalamazoo
Lake County
Lansing
Lathrup Village
Meridian Twp
Muskegon County
Pontiac
Southfield
Troy

Minnesota
Duluth
Minneapolis
Robbinsdale
St. Paul

Mississippi
Jackson

Missouri
Kansas City
St. Louis
University City

Nebraska
Lincoln

Nevada
Elko
Elko County
Las Vegas
Silver City
Sparks

New Hampshire
Exeter
Farmington
Marlborough
Peterborough
Portsmouth

New Jersey
Englewood
Ewing
Franklin Twp
Highland Park
Keansburg
Lawrence Twp
Mercer County
Montclair Twp
Mullica
New Brunswick
Passaic County
Paterson
Phillipsburg
Plainfield
Princeton
South Brunswick
West Windsor
Willingboro

New Mexico
Albuquerque
Aztec
Bayard
Farmington
Grant County
Las Vegas
Los Alamos County
Rio Arriba County
Santa Fe
Silver City
Socorro
Taos
Valencia County

New York
Albany
Albany County
Bethlehem Twp
Brighton
Canton
Danby
Elmira
Greenburgh
Huntington
Ithaca
Mamaroneck
Mount Vernon
Town of New Paltz
Village of New Paltz
New York
N. Hempstead
Nyack
Plattsburgh

Rosendale
Rochester
St. Lawrence County
Schenectady
Schuyler County
Syracuse
Tompkins County
Urbana
Westchester County
Woodstock

North Carolina
Boone
Carrboro
Chapel Hill
Davidson
Durham
Durham County
Greensboro
Orange County
Raleigh

Ohio
Cleveland Heights
Oberlin
Oxford
Toledo
Yellow Springs

Oregon
Ashland
Astoria
Benton County
Coos County
Corvallis
Douglas County
Eugene
Gaston
Lane County
Multnomah County
Port Orford
Portland
Talent
Wheeler

Pennsylvania
Berks County
Erie
Lansdowne
Philadelphia
Pittsburgh
Reading
State College
Wilkinsburg
Yeadon
York

Rhode Island
Bristol
Charlestown
Middletown

New Shoreham
N. Providence
Providence
S. Kingstown

South Carolina
Columbia

South Dakota
Rapid City

Tennessee
Blount County

Texas
Austin
Dallas
El Paso
Sunset Valley
Wichita Falls

Utah
Castle Valley

Virginia
Alexandria
Arlington County
Charlottesville
Falls Church
Richmond

Washington
Bainbridge Island
Bellingham
Clallam County
Coupeville
Jefferson County
King County
Olympia
Oroville
Port Townsend
Riverside
San Juan County
Seattle
Snoqualmie
Tacoma
Tonasket
Tumwater
Twisp
Vashon-Maury Island
Whatcom County

Washington, D.C.

West Virginia
Huntington

Wisconsin
Douglas County
Eau Claire
Madison
Milwaukee

Wyoming
Fremont County

that is at odds with our Constitution, we will have handed a definitive victory to our enemies by allowing unchecked police power to triumph over individual rights and the rule of law in this country. At that point, our government will be no better than the dictatorships we have for so long opposed on principled grounds.

In a Jan. 2003 interview with the *Los Angeles Times*, constitutional law professor Jonathan Turley remarked, "Since 9/11, the Constitution has gone from an objective to be satisfied to an obstacle to national defense. . . . As these changes mount, at what point do we become something other than a free and democratic nation?" Americans would do well to heed the warning behind Turley's words: with every piece of Patriot Act–type legislation that Congress passes, our basic constitutional protections are being undermined and we are, indeed, moving further away from being a free and democratic nation.

To quote a recent editorial, "Is this how liberty dies?" For the sake of this great nation, I hope not.

EVALUATING THE AUTHOR'S ARGUMENTS:

In the viewpoint you just read, the author argues that the federal government invades Americans' privacy under provisions of the Patriot Act. In the following viewpoint, the author contends that the U.S. government practices restraint under the Patriot Act and does not invade Americans' privacy. After reading both viewpoints, which perspective do you find more convincing? Explain your reasoning.

The Patriot Act Does Not Violate Americans' Privacy

Heather Mac Donald

"The act carefully preserves the traditional checks and balances that safeguard civil liberties; . . . not a single abuse of government power has been found or even alleged."

In the following viewpoint author Heather Mac Donald argues that modestly expanded powers under the Patriot Act have not been used to violate Americans' privacy. Mac Donald reports that not a single abuse of government power has been found or alleged. She points out that some of the Patriot Act provisions are laws that have already been in effect for decades, such as delaying notification of a search. Mac Donald says that anti–Patriot Act leaders' biggest issue is that the government acts in secret, but because secrecy is the most important factor in terrorism investigations, publicizing and giving advance notification of a search is not an effective way to protect the country, in her opinion. She believes that too many past restrictions on intelligence gathering compromised Americans' public safety. Mac Donald

Heather Mac Donald, "Testimony: Oversight Hearing on the Patriot Act," Manhattan Institute for Policy Research, May 3, 2005. Reproduced by permission of the author.

concludes that the Patriot Act allows intelligence analysts to gather information needed to fight terrorism while protecting Americans' civil liberties.

Mac Donald is a John M. Olin Fellow at the Manhattan Institute, a political think tank that promotes reform in various areas of public policy.

AS YOU READ, CONSIDER THE FOLLOWING QUESTIONS:

1. What does the author say is the most powerful weapon against terrorism, and how does this relate to the Patriot Act?
2. According to the author, what is wrong with criticisms of Section 213 of the Patriot Act?
3. What is needed to track down terrorist-related Islamic activity, in the author's opinion?

T he most powerful weapon against terrorism is intelligence. The United States is too big a country to rely on physical barriers against attack; the most certain defense is advanced knowledge of terrorist plans.

The Patriot Act Modestly Expands Government Power

In recognition of this fact, Congress amended existing surveillance powers after 9/11 to ready them for the terrorist challenge. The signal achievement of these amendments, known as the Patriot Act, was to tear down the regulatory "wall" that had prevented anti-terrorism intelligence agents and anti-terrorism criminal agents from sharing information. The Patriot Act made other necessary changes to surveillance law as well: it extended to terrorism investigators powers long enjoyed by criminal investigators, and it brought surveillance law into the 21st century of cell phones and e-mail. Where the act modestly expands the government's authority, it does so for one reason only: to make sure that the government can gather enough information to prevent terrorism, not just prosecute it after the fact.

Each modest expansion of government power in the Patriot Act is accompanied by the most effective restraint in our constitutional system: judicial review. The act carefully preserves the traditional checks and balances that safeguard civil liberties; four years after its enactment, after constant monitoring by the Justice Department's Inspector General and a host of hostile advocacy groups, not a single abuse of government power has been found or even alleged.

This record of restraint is not the picture of the act most often presented in the media or by government critics, however. The Patriot Act has been the target of the most successful disinformation campaign in recent memory. From the day of its passage, law enforcement critics have portrayed it as an unprecedented power grab by an administration intent on trampling civil rights. . . .

Section 213 of the Patriot Act Does Not Abuse Power

Section 213 carefully balances traditional expectations of notice and the imperatives of preemptive terror and crime investigations. That's not how left- and right-wing libertarians have portrayed it, however. They present Section 213, which they have dubbed "sneak-and-peek," as one of the most outrageous new powers seized by former Attorney General John Ashcroft. The ACLU's [American Civil Liberties Union] fund-raising pitches warn: "Now, the government can secretly enter your home while you're away . . . rifle through your personal belongings . . . download your computer files . . . and seize any items at will. . . . And, because of the Patriot Act, you may never know what the government has done."

Notice the ACLU's "Now." Like every anti-213 crusader, the ACLU implies that Section 213 is a radical new power. This charge is a rank fabrication. For decades, federal courts have allowed investigators to delay notice of a search in drug cases, organized crime, and child pornography, for the same reasons as in Section 213. Indeed, the ability to delay notice of a search is an almost inevitable concomitant of investigations that seek to stop a crime before it happens. But the lack of precise uniformity in the court rulings on delayed notice slowed down complex national terror cases. Section 213 codified existing case law under a single national standard to streamline detective work; it did not create new authority regarding searches. Those critics who believe that the target of a search should always be notified prior to the search, regardless of the risks, should have raised their complaints decades ago—to the Supreme Court and the many other courts who have recognized the necessity of a delay option.

Critics of Section 213 raise the spectre of widespread surveillance abuse should the government be allowed to delay notice. FBI agents will be rummaging around the effects of law-abiding citizens on mere whim, even stealing from them, allege the anti-Patriot propagandists. But the government has had the delayed notice power for decades, and the anti-Patriot demagogues have not brought forward a single case of abuse under delayed notice case law. Their argument against Section 213 remains purely speculative: It *could* be abused. But there's no need to speculate; the historical record refutes the claim.

The Patriot Act Contains Judicial Review Provisions

The most pervasive tactic used against the Patriot Act is to conceal its judicial review provisions.

The cascades of anti-Section 213 vitriol contain not one mention of the fact that the FBI can only delay notice of a search pursuant to judicial approval. It is a federal judge who decides whether a delay is reasonable, not law enforcement officials. And before a government agent can even seek to delay notice of a search, he must already have proven to a judge that he has probable cause to conduct the search in the first place. . . .

Anti-Patriot lore has it that Section 213 allows the government to permanently conceal a search. The section "allows the government to conduct secret searches without notification," cries Richard Leone, president of the Century Foundation and editor of *The War on Our Freedoms; Civil Liberties in an Age of Terrorism*. This conceit rewrites the section, which provides only for a delay of notice, not its cancellation. A warrant issued under Section 213 must explicitly require notice after a "reasonable" period of time. This key feature of the section is completely suppressed by the critics.

Secrecy Is Needed to Catch Terrorists

Many of the attacks on the Patriot Act emanate from a single source: the critics do not believe that the government should ever act in secret. Recipients of document production orders in terror investigations —whether Section 215 orders or national security letters under the 1986 Electronic Communications Privacy Act—should be able to

John Ashcroft, former United States attorney general, displays a copy of an overview of the Patriot Act at a press conference. The overview supported proponents of the act by claiming its key strategies did not infringe on civil liberties.

publicize the government's request, say the critics. If intelligence agents want to search a suspected cell's apartment, they should inform the cell members in advance to give them an opportunity to challenge the search. Time and again, law enforcement critics disparage the Foreign Intelligence Surveillance Court, because its proceedings are closed to the public.

This transparent approach may satisfy those on the left and right who believe that the American people have no greater enemy than their own government, but it fails to answer the major question: how would it possibly be effective in protecting the country? The Patriot Act critics fail to grasp the distinction between the prosecution of an already committed crime, for which probable cause and publicity requirements were crafted, and the effort to preempt a catastrophic attack on American soil before it happens. For preemptive investigations, secrecy is of the essence. Opponents of the Patriot Act have never explained how they think the government can track down the web of Islamist activity in public. Given the fact that Section 213 and other sections are carefully circumscribed with judicial checks and balances, it is in fact the secrecy that they allow that most riles the opponents.

The Patriot Act Protects Civil Liberties and Protects the United States Against Terrorism

The recent history of government intelligence-gathering belies the notion that any government surveillance power sets us on a slippery slope to tyranny. There *is* a slippery-slope problem in terror investigations—but it runs the other way. Since the 1970s, libertarians of all political stripes have piled restriction after restriction on intelligence-gathering, even preventing two antiterror FBI agents in the same office from collaborating on a case if one was an "intelligence" investigator and the other a "criminal" investigator. By the late '90s, the bureau worried more about avoiding a pseudo–civil liberties scandal than about preventing a terror attack. No one demanding the ever-more Byzantine protections against hypothetical abuse asked whether they were exacting a cost in public safety. We know now that they were. . . .

In conclusion, the Patriot Act is a balanced updating of surveillance authority in light of the new reality of catastrophic terrorism. It corrects anachronisms in law enforcement powers, whereby health care fraud investigators, for example, enjoyed greater ability to gather evidence than Al Qaeda intelligence squads. It created no novel powers, but built on existing authorities within the context of constitutional checks and balances. It protects civil liberties while making sure that intelligence analysts can get the information they need to protect the country. The law should be reenacted.

EVALUATING THE AUTHOR'S ARGUMENTS:

In this viewpoint Mac Donald contends that the Patriot Act utilizes a system of checks and balances that protects Americans' civil liberties. What pieces of evidence does she provide to support her claim? Did she convince you of her argument? Explain why or why not.

The Powers Granted in the Patriot Act Have Been Abused

David Weigel

"As scandal piled on top of scandal, it became harder, then impossible, to deny that the powers granted to the executive could be abused by some corrupt actors or by agencies."

In the following viewpoint author David Weigel cites several cases in which U.S. government agencies have abused powers granted under the Patriot Act. Weigel accuses the FBI of using its new powers to mail thousands of National Security Letters to people who were not part of ongoing investigations and without using other options first—a direct violation of U.S. citizens' civil liberties. He also points out that, because of new powers granted under the Patriot Act, the Department of Justice was able to dismiss eight proficient U.S. attorneys without having to obtain congressional approval for their replacements. Weigel contends that the Patriot Act was passed as a quick response to the 9/11 attacks, but because the new laws have resulted in numerous scandals, it is no longer supported by politicians or American

David Weigel, "Right All Along, Unfortunately: The 'Chicken Littles' Win the Civil Liberties Debate," *Reason*, vol. 39, June 2007, pp. 12–13. Copyright © 2007 by Reason Foundation, 3415 S. Sepulveda Blvd., Suite 400, Los Angeles, CA 90034, www.reason.com. Reproduced by permission.

citizens. He concludes that the Patriot Act does not make America secure, and that it was not the right law to pass.

Weigel is an associate editor of Reason.com and *Reason* magazine. He writes frequently on politics and lives in Washington, D.C.

AS YOU READ, CONSIDER THE FOLLOWING QUESTIONS:

1. During what year did the FBI send out thousands of National Security Letters, according to the author?
2. What does the phrase "Chicken Littles" mean in the context of the viewpoint?
3. Name at least three scandals the author says prove the government abuses powers granted in the Patriot Act.

Attorney General Alberto Gonzales and Federal Bureau of Investigation Director Robert Mueller spent much of March [2007] doing something neither man was used to doing: apologizing. On March 10, Mueller admitted that the agency hadn't told the truth about its uses of PATRIOT Act powers to investigate Americans, admitting that nearly 50,000 privacy-busting "National Security Letters" had been sent in 2005 instead of the 30,000 Congress had been told of. Three days later, Gonzales walked the same plank to confess that the Department of Justice may have lied to Congress about the reasons why eight U.S. Attorneys had been dismissed and replaced with less-experienced drones who'd be more willing to investigate Democrats.

Mixed Feelings About the Patriot Act

Six and a half years earlier, Cassandras [those with prophetic insight] who warned about abuses like these couldn't get a hearing in Washington. Only one U.S. senator, the Wisconsin Democrat Russ Feingold, opposed the PATRIOT Act in October 2001. Only 47 senators voted against the White House's drive to close debate on PATRIOT Act reauthorization on December 16, 2005—enough to delay the vote, but not enough to force major changes. But on March 20, 2007: 94 senators voted to repeal the PATRIOT provision that let the Department of Justice fire U.S. attorneys and replace them without new nomination hearings.

In the wake of the 9/11 attacks, citizens and legislators alike were quick to go along with the idea that government needed sweeping new powers—and less oversight—if it was going to defend us against terrorism. It was this idea that gave us Gitmo [the terrorist prison camp at Guantánamo Bay], warrantless wiretaps, the PATRIOT Act, and the Department of Homeland Security. The idea faced critics from the start, but for a long time, most of Congress was willing to meet those criticisms with faith: faith in the president, faith in legal authorities, faith in agents' pumped-up powers in the field.

Those Who Worried About the Patriot Act Were Right

That first lopsided Senate battle over the PATRIOT Act set the tone. The administration mollified skeptical U.S. senators with small changes to a bill that began as a K-Tel[1] compilation of new state powers: The attorney general would still be allowed to seize education records, for example, but now he was required to present some reasons for doing so. Feingold, who proposed several doomed amendments to the law, was the only senator to break faith with the parties and vote against the entire bill.

"I came to feel that the administration's demand for haste was inappropriate; indeed, it was dangerous," Feingold told a Milwaukee audience after the vote. He worried that "the bill contains some very significant changes in criminal procedure that will apply to every federal criminal investigation in this country, not just those involving terrorism."

In other words, Feingold foresaw many of the problems that would emerge as federal investigations clashed with Americans' civil rights. At every turn, security hawks have argued their critics are overanxious, paranoid "Chicken Littles." At this point, the chickens are looking awfully prescient. It's the hawks who are in trouble, beset by scandals connected directly to the laws for which they begged.

The scandals began to percolate early in 2002, but none of them stuck; complaints about government snooping in library records and

---

[1]K-Tel International is best known for its compilation music albums, such as *The Super Hits* series and *The Number One Hits* series.

In March 2007 FBI inspector general Glenn Fine appeared before the Senate Judiciary Committee where he testified that the FBI had abused its new powers granted by the Patriot Act.

among antiwar groups may have gotten some buzz online and in local newspapers, but not in Congress. The first story that did was the revelation in late 2005 that the White House was approving phone wiretaps without getting warrants from the special courts created by the Foreign Intelligence Surveillance Act. The *New York Times* reported this in December 2005, just as the U.S. Senate was debating whether to reauthorize the PATRIOT Act and extend provisions that had been set to expire.

Mishandling of the Patriot Act Reauthorization Process

Civil liberties watchdogs, whose numbers had swelled since 2001, saw the revelations as a confirmation of their worst fears, and PATRIOT reauthorization became a tougher sell. According to Sen. John Sununu (R-N.H.), what really outraged senators wasn't the scandal itself so much as Attorney General Alberto Gonzales' refusal to meet with them to discuss the PATRIOT Act, the expiring provisions, and various related issues.

"The way they handled the reauthorization process was horrible," says Sununu, who went on to filibuster the reauthorization. "The attorney general had an opportunity to develop a rapport with Congress. That's what we wanted. He decided not to engage in discussions. In my opinion, that was the failure that led to the confrontation."

Abusing the New Powers

One point of contention between senators and the White House was National Security Letters, documents that compel their targets to release any and all information the FBI requests from them; all the FBI need assert is that the request is somehow related to a terrorism investigation. Under the PATRIOT Act, their use expanded enormously. After watching the FBI send its reported 30,000 letters in 2005 Sununu (as part of the PATRIOT reauthorization compromise) passed a law requiring oversight by the Inspector General's Office and reports to Congress on how the letters are being used.

© 2007 John Trever, *The Albuquerque Journal*, and PoliticalCartoons.com.

That earned scorching criticisms from other Republicans, who accused Sununu, Feingold, and other critics of making an issue out of thin air. "The threat to Americans' liberty today," Viet Dinh, one of the lawyers who crafted the PATRIOT Act, said in a 2006 debate with former Rep. Bob Barr, "comes from Al Qaeda and its associates and the people who would destroy America and her people, not the brave men and women who work to defend this country!"

In March 2007, FBI Inspector General Glenn Fine released a report that undermined that argument. It turned out the bureau had underreported the number of requests for National Security Letters, had issued letters before exhausting other options, and had issued them to Americans who were not the targets of ongoing investigations. In short, the FBI had abused its new powers.

"That vindicated my concerns over that provision of the PATRIOT Act," says Sen. Larry Craig, an Idaho Republican who had joined Sununu and most Democrats in the 2005 filibuster. "Not because I have reason to believe that FBI agents were acting with ill intent, but it does show that we shouldn't create shortcuts when it comes to civil rights. Mistakes will, and did, happen."

Investigating Democrats Was a Misuse of Power

That scandal was soon chased from the headlines by something even more incendiary: The White House had fired eight competent U.S. attorneys for, among other things, not working hard enough to prosecute Democrats. Washington State's John McKay hadn't dug into claims of Democratic voter fraud in a governor's race; New Mexico's David Iglesias, the model for Tom Cruise's character in *A Few Good Men*, wasn't willing to rush an indictment against a Democratic state senator before an election. And the power that let the president replace them with cronies was enshrined in the PATRIOT Act.

Presidents had always set up a revolving door for the U.S. attorneys at the starts of their terms, and they had the right to shuffle them out and nominate new blood at any time. But PATRIOT effectively eliminated Congress' role in approving those replacements, by removing restrictions on the length of service for interim U.S. attorneys and allowed them to serve indefinitely without confirmation by the Senate. At first liberals, then conservatives started calling for the attorney general to fall on his sword, [and] the Senate voted to strip the president of that power.

Passing the Patriot Act Was Not the Right Thing to Do

It took its time, but the political class has finally lost confidence in its belief that the government had done the right things to secure America after 9/11. As scandal piled on top of scandal, it became harder, then impossible, to deny that the powers granted to the executive could be abused by some corrupt actors or by agencies enamored of their own secrecy.

This impacts the way Washingtonians play out the decade's big hypothetical scenario: What happens if we get hit again? How will politics change after another 9/11? The thinking had been that politics would pivot right back to the frenzied "whatever my government wants" attitude of 2001. But the validation of civil libertarians' fears has changed all that.

"This is a case where I can say 'I was right all along,'" says Sununu. "But I am not happy about it."

EVALUATING THE AUTHOR'S ARGUMENTS:

David Weigel quotes from several sources to support the points he makes in his essay. Make a list of everyone he quotes, including their qualifications and the nature of their comments. Then, analyze his sources—are they credible? Are they well qualified to speak on this subject?

The Powers Granted in the Patriot Act Have Not Been Abused

Stuart Taylor Jr.

"This power is undeniably sweeping. But it is almost certainly constitutional."

In the following viewpoint author Stuart Taylor Jr. argues that powers issued under the Patriot Act are constitutional and have not been abused. Taylor contends that although the Patriot Act laws are sweeping they are legal and constitutional. He points out that for decades courts have maintained secrecy in order to conduct successful investigations, and prosecutors have always had extensive powers to subpoena library and medical records relevant to criminal investigations—these laws are not specific to the Patriot Act. Taylor states that only a few provisions under the Patriot Act have provoked controversy. In his opinion, this controversy has allowed the Patriot Act to be scrutinized very closely and changed where needed. He suggests that problems contained in the Patriot Act are mild and can be fixed by making modest revisions. In conclusion, Taylor states that the Patriot Act is not a threat to Americans' civil liberties and that it is a good law overall.

Stuart Taylor Jr. is a senior columnist and writer for the *National Journal*, a weekly magazine that reports on U.S. policy and politics.

AS YOU READ, CONSIDER THE FOLLOWING QUESTIONS:

1. How many states have passed anti–Patriot Act measures, as reported by the author?
2. According to the author, how many Patriot Act provisions are considered highly controversial?
3. Why is Section 215 called the "library" provision, according to Taylor?

"When the Bush administration says it wants to make permanent the freedom-stealing provisions of the PATRIOT Act, they're telling those of us who believe in privacy, due process, and the right to dissent that it's time to surrender our freedom."

So screams the first sentence of a recent fundraising letter from the American Civil Liberties Union. This and countless other overheated attacks—from conservative libertarians and gun-rights activists as well as liberal groups—have scared some 375 local governments and states into passing anti–PATRIOT Act measures, while sending earnest librarians into a panic about Big Brother snooping into library borrowers' reading habits.

But consider what the ACLU says when it is seeking to be taken seriously by people who know something about the issues: "Most of the voluminous PATRIOT Act is actually unobjectionable from a civil-liberties point of view, and . . . the law makes important changes that give law enforcement agents the tools they need to protect against terrorist attacks."

That's right: That was the ACLU talking, in an April 5 press release. To be sure, the release goes on to stress that "a few provisions . . . unnecessarily trample civil liberties, and must be revised." Well, perhaps. And with 16 provisions of the USA PA-TRIOT Act scheduled to sunset on December 31 it is surely time to give the entire 342-page, 156-section law the careful scrutiny that it has not received from most of the legislators who passed it in October 2001.

This is not to deny that the Bush administration has engaged in grave abuses, both at home and abroad, beginning with its unduly prolonged post-9/11 detention and (in many cases) abuse of hundreds of visitors from the Muslim world. Most alarming have been the administration's claims of near-dictatorial wartime powers to seize and interrogate—even to the point of torture—anyone in the world whom the president labels an "enemy combatant."

But contrary to many a newspaper account, these abuses and overreaching claims of power had nothing to with the PATRIOT Act, about which so many people have cried wolf that the real wolves have received less attention than they deserve.

The good news is that with the December 31 sunset approaching, serious thinking has penetrated the previously shallow debate. Anyone interested in reading the best arguments for and against the more controversial provisions can find them at www.PatriotDebates.com, a collection of mini-debates among an ideologically diverse group of 17 experts. The "sourceblog" was put together by Stewart Baker, chair of the American Bar Association's Standing Committee on Law and National Security.

"In several cases, the civil libertarians we recruited to find fault with particular provisions have ended up proposing modification rather than repeal," writes Baker. And amid numerous suggestions for modest tinkering, it turns out that only about six provisions have provoked very spirited debate. This should not be surprising: Much of the act consists of long-overdue amendments—which were on the Clinton Justice Department's wish list well before 9/11—to give government agents pursuing terrorists and spies the same investigative tools that are available to those pursuing ordinary criminals, and to counteract the bad guys' use of new technologies such as e-mail and disposable cellphones.

The most widely denounced provision is Section 215, one of the 16 that will sunset unless reenacted. It is commonly known as the "library" provision because it might someday be used to obtain library records—even though, as the Justice Department reported on April 5, it never has been so used and does not even contain the word "library." Section 215 authorizes the FBI to obtain an order from a special court, established under the Foreign Intelligence Surveillance Act, to require any business or other entity to surrender any records or other "tangible things" that the FBI claims to be relevant to an intelligence investigation.

This power is undeniably sweeping.

But it is almost certainly constitutional under Supreme Court rulings that allow, for example, the government to see your credit card records. And it is far less invasive of privacy than, say, a wiretap. What many critics ignore is that for decades, prosecutors have had even more-sweeping powers to issue subpoenas requiring businesses and organizations, including libraries and medical facilities, to hand over any records that are arguably relevant to ordinary criminal investigations. Such subpoenas have been routinely issued without prior judicial scrutiny for many years.

Critics complain that a Section 215 order can apply to records pertaining to people not suspected of being foreign agents. (The same is true of an ordinary subpoena.) But this is as it should be. A key technique for catching terrorists is to trace their activities through those of associates who are not themselves engaged, or known to be engaged, in terrorist activities.

This is not to say that Section 215 is flawless. Most obviously, it fails to specify any way for a recipient of an unwarranted or overly broad order to ask a court to reject or narrow the order. Even Attorney General Alberto Gonzales has conceded that this is a defect that should be cured.

Gonzales, in this and other ways, including his April 13 meeting with ACLU Executive Director Anthony Romero, has responded to critics far more constructively than his predecessor, John Ashcroft, ever did.

Critics, including Peter Swire, a law professor at Ohio State University who is the Section 215 critic on PatriotDebates.com, also make a strong case that a gag-order provision in Section 215 is unduly sweeping. This provision automatically bars recipients from disclosing Section 215 orders to the media or to anyone else, ever. The purpose is to prevent terrorists from learning that the government is on their trail. But the absolute and perpetual nature of the gag orders eliminates a key check on possible abuse. Swire proposes

Supporters of the Patriot Act, such as former attorney general Alberto Gonzales (pictured), have conceded that flaws do exist in the act but argue that its core laws are instrumental to intelligence sharing and are ultimately essential in combating terrorism.

several limitations. At least one seems worthy of adoption: The gag orders should expire after six months unless extended by the FISA court.

The other major target of civil libertarians is Section 213, which authorizes so-called "sneak-and-peek" warrants for what the government calls "delayed-notice" searches. Ordinarily, search warrants must be served on the subjects at the time of a search. Section 213, which is not among the provisions scheduled to sunset, recognizes several exceptions, allowing judges to delay notice of a search until after a search is already completed, when the government shows that delay may be necessary to avoid: 1) endangering life or physical safety, 2) flight from prosecution, 3) tampering with evidence, 4) intimidation of witnesses, or 5) "otherwise seriously jeopardizing an investigation or unduly delaying a trial." This last is the so-called catch-all provision.

Amid a deluge of misleading scare rhetoric about FBI agents rummaging through bedrooms and covering their tracks, most critics have ignored the fact that Section 213's main impact is to codify what courts have done for decades when necessary to avoid blowing the secrecy that is critical to some investigations.

Critics complain that Section 213 was enacted under a false flag, because sneak-and-peek searches in terrorism investigations had already been authorized by FISA. The provision's main impact, they say, has been to make it easier for agents to obtain sneak-and-peek warrants in ordinary criminal investigations. This is true. It's also true that a strong case can be made for revising Section 213 to require notice of an ordinary criminal-investigation search within, say, seven days unless the court authorizes further delay. And it's arguable that the catchall provision makes it too easy to get a sneak-and-peek warrant.

But on the scale of threats to liberty, Section 213 ranks far, far below such widely ignored laws as, for example, the five-year mandatory minimum prison sentence for possessing five grams of crack cocaine.

The debates over the other four most controversial provisions—which cover three subject areas: "roving wiretaps," information-sharing between criminal and intelligence investigators, and prosecutions of people for providing terrorists with "material support"—also boil down to plausible arguments for and against relatively modest adjustments in the liberty-security balance.

Many libertarians have united behind the proposed SAFE Act, a package of revisions that would probably be of no great harm to the war on terrorism and no great benefit to civil liberties. But at a time of domestic security threats more dire than in any period since the Civil War—threats posed by jihadists who have a chillingly realistic hope of buying or making doomsday weapons that could kill us by the millions—most of these proposals strike me as small steps in the wrong direction.

But even if I'm incorrect about that, the big news is that for all the Sturm und Drang, we may be seeing the emergence of a remarkable expert consensus: For the most part, the USA PATRIOT Act is a good law.

EVALUATING THE AUTHOR'S ARGUMENTS:

In the viewpoint you just read, the author argues that the Patriot Act is a good law that does not allow abuse of powers. In the previous viewpoint, the author contends that powers used under the Patriot Act are invasive and have been abused. After reading both viewpoints, which argument do you find more persuasive and why? Explain your reasoning.

Chapter 3

Who Is Threatened by the Patriot Act?

Many Americans are concerned about the effect of the Patriot Act on the nation's libraries.

Viewpoint

1

Libraries and Their Patrons Are Threatened by the Patriot Act

Emily Drabinski

"If a user suspects that her reading habits will be tracked, [her] access to information is fundamentally abridged."

In the following viewpoint author Emily Drabinski argues that the Patriot Act violates library patrons' right to privacy. She contends that the Patriot Act allows the FBI to seize patrons' records without having to obtain a judge's approval. Furthermore, the library receiving the subpoena for records must not disclose that they have received the order. Drabinski argues that this gag order law is the most restrictive in the history of library surveillance programs. Drabinski urges librarians to organize and devise strategies to oppose the Patriot Act in order to protect their patrons' privacy, preserve intellectual freedom, and safeguard readers' right to free inquiry.

Drabinski is a reference and instruction librarian at Sarah Lawrence College in New York.

Emily Drabinski, "Librarians and the Patriot Act," *Radical Teacher*, winter 2006, pp. 12–15. Reproduced by permission.

AS YOU READ, CONSIDER THE FOLLOWING QUESTIONS:

1. According to the author, what is important about Section 505 of the Patriot Act?

2. What is the name of the library monitoring program enacted in the 1980s, and how does it factor into the author's argument?

3. Name at least three actions the author says librarians have taken to resist the Patriot Act.

In 2003, Santa Cruz County library director Anne Turner proclaimed to her board of directors that the FBI "has not been here this month." An odd pronouncement, except in the context of the Patriot Act, which forbids librarians to tell anyone if the FBI has requested patron records. By making their absence explicit, Turner can get around the gag order—if she says nothing, the board will know the FBI has invaded the privacy of a patron. Turner is only one among many librarians galvanized into action since the October 2001 passage of the Patriot Act. This article addresses the effects of the Patriot Act on library professionals, documents our resistance efforts, and suggests that the maintenance of our profession requires a broader resistance to political and economic forces. . . .

The Role of Privacy in the Library

Libraries enjoy a unique place in the public imagination: they are perhaps the only publicly funded institution people actually like. Unlike the rest of twenty-first century America, the library does not seek to maximize profit or develop markets. The library is a noncoercive public space where books, movies, music—the stuff of ideas and of entertainment—are purchased with collective funds and then shared in kind among members of the community. Ideally—though not always, in practice—it doesn't matter in a library who you are or where you come from. Once over the threshold, all are free and equal members of a human community, with free and equal access to the sum of human knowledge. While different in some key respects, school, university, and public libraries share these essential values.

The right to free inquiry relies on a right to privacy. If a user suspects that her reading habits will be tracked, [her] access to information is fundamentally abridged. Libraries respond materially to this demand. Automated circulation systems are built to erase patron borrowing records as soon as materials are returned, and our code of professional ethics makes our commitment to patron privacy explicit.

The Patriot Act Violates Readers' Privacy

While the Patriot Act and other post-9/11 legislation have had repressive consequences throughout society, Sections 215 and 505 of that Act are directly relevant to libraries, in that they directly and explicitly abridge the right to patron privacy. Section 215 amends the Foreign Intelligence Surveillance Act of 1978 to expand the range of material objects that may be legally obtained in a search by federal agents. Section 215 allows for the seizure of any "tangible thing," a delimitation of the 1978 legislation that allows for the seizure of borrowing records as well as records of Internet activity in a public library. This provision was to sunset in March 2006. The reauthorization language demands that the FBI present "reasonable grounds" for the assumption that the records are "relevant," and demands that any

In order to maintain the free-inquiry atmosphere of America's libraries, librarians are battling the Patriot Act's provisions that allow the FBI full access to patrons' records.

seizure order describe the records sought. While these are welcome changes, they do not fundamentally alter the right of law enforcement to seize patron records.

Section 505 of the Patriot Act of 2001 represents an additional federal intrusion on privacy rights. This section amended three federal statutes to extend the use of National Security Letters (NSLs) to libraries. NSLs are used to subpoena information without requiring that the agent bring evidence before a judge. Reauthorization language in 2006 releases libraries from compliance with NSLs when they are "functioning in their traditional roles." However, libraries are still subject to NSLs when they provide Internet service to users.

Gag Orders for Librarians

A particularly insidious aspect of the Patriot Act for libraries is the mandate that librarians served with subpoenas or NSLs keep the information requests secret. The original legislation prevented librarians from telling anyone that information had been requested. Reauthorization language in sections 215 and 505 reform that language to allow disclosure to "any person to whom disclosure is necessary to comply with such order," and allows recipients to obtain legal counsel in order to comply. While these changes may be some comfort to librarians, they are no comfort at all to patrons. If your borrowing records or records of your Internet activity are requested, it is illegal for anyone to tell you.

> **FAST FACT**
>
> Forty-seven of the 342 pages of the USA PATRIOT Act apply to law enforcement's ability to acquire communications related to terrorism that take place within libraries.

The gag order also works against organizing among librarians. In his discussion of the Library Awareness Program, a monitoring program dating to the 1980s, Herbert Foerstel [former head of branch libraries at the University of Maryland] notes that the atmosphere engendered by the Patriot Act is worse than previous library surveillance programs because of its secrecy: "We know the chilling possibilities that these new authorities represent, but they will be more difficult to document and assess because of the unprecedented 'gag order' that

© 2006 Bob Englehart, *The Hartford Courant*, and PoliticalCartoons.com.

the Patriot Act imposes on librarians, booksellers, and others served with the newly authorized secret warrants." We can't talk to each other about any warrants we might receive, and so are limited in our ability to conceptualize the extent of the warrants. How can we know the extent of the problem when we are prohibited from speaking freely about it?

Librarians Challenge the Patriot Act

Resistance by librarians has taken many forms, including local actions meant to inform patrons about the abridgement of their rights. Librarians in Santa Cruz posted signs warning patrons that the Patriot Act "prohibits library workers from informing you if federal agents have obtained records about you." Similar signs were posted by librarians in Killington, Vermont, and Skokie, Illinois, and librarian-activist Jessamyn West offered a number of print-and-post signs on her blog, librarian.net. Santa Cruz librarians also began a policy of shredding documents daily, telling the *New York Times* that "the basic strategy now is to keep as little historical information as possible." The American Library Association website has collated a number of brochures and signs to distribute from New York City to Nampa, Idaho, and provides a hotline librarians can call if they receive section 215 subpoenas or NSLs.

Librarians have also challenged parts of the Patriot Act in court. Most famously, in *Doe v. Gonzalez*, four Connecticut librarians challenged the gag order embedded in section 505 of the Patriot Act. The government eventually dropped their demand for secrecy, and the librarians have since discussed their frustration at their inability to contest government claims that library records were safe under the Patriot Act.

The American Library Association (ALA) is also heavily involved with lobbying and legislative efforts, and has worked in both the House and the Senate to introduce bills that would remove library records from the set of documents that may be seized under the Patriot Act. None of this legislation has moved out of committee.

Librarians Support Intellectual Freedom

What accounts for librarians' organized and rapid opposition to the Patriot Act, beyond our structural support for privacy rights? For one thing, our institutional history of activism around intellectual freedom has produced institutional structures that channel opposition to specific kinds of abridgements of information access, including censorship and surveillance efforts. The ALA's Office for Intellectual Freedom coordinates the profession's resistance efforts through the Freedom to Read Foundation; round-tables and committees focused on local, state, national, and international conflicts over intellectual freedom; and the Intellectual Freedom Action Network, an electronic grassroots-activist listserv that generates rapid response from the professional community to threats against intellectual freedom.

There are, however, fundamental limits to a strategy of resistance that is essentially reactive and narrow in focus. While librarians respond quickly and effectively to challenges posed by the Patriot Act, we have little in the way of sustained resistance to systemic forces that undermine information equity and access in less visible but more fundamental ways. An assessment of our resistance to the Patriot Act gives us an opportunity to examine how librarians could cultivate a broader strategy of resistance to forces that threaten the basic values of our profession. . . .

Librarians Must Take Action

Librarians can and do organize against government and corporate abridgements of our core professional values. Some of this activism is easy to identify. Librarians post anti–Patriot Act signs in our libraries, file lawsuits against the federal government for violating our privacy, and send letters and petitions to our congressional representatives decrying legislation that limits information access. Some of our activism is simply a part of our daily labor. As we produce information systems that actually erase data as a way to prevent surveillance, and work to develop more efficient systems for sharing information, we are working against government and economic forces that limit information access.

EVALUATING THE AUTHOR'S ARGUMENTS:

Emily Drabinski suggests that librarians should actively resist government surveillance of library records. What do you think? Should librarians take measures to prevent the government from obtaining data from libraries, or should they cooperate with federal investigations? Explain your position.

Libraries and Their Patrons Are Not Threatened by the Patriot Act

Michael B. Mukasey

"What about the section the librarians were so concerned about, Section 215? Well, it bears some mention that the word library appears nowhere in that section."

In the following viewpoint, author Michael B. Mukasey argues that people overreact to the Patriot Act, especially librarians who claim it threatens their patrons. He argues that Patriot Act provisions that allow authorities to gather business records and conduct electronic surveillance are similar to existing investigative techniques that allow investigators access to telephone records and use of roving wiretaps. Mukasey argues that although Section 215 is of great concern to librarians because it allows the FBI to issue subpoenas to seize records, it is a good law because investigators are able to gather good evidence to prosecute dangerous criminals. In fact, Mukasey points out that access to library records was critical in the capture of one of America's most famous terrorists, Ted Kaczynski. Mukasey concludes that the Patriot Act provides a good balance between library patrons' rights and law enforcement's needs, and says that people would not have as many misconceptions about the Patriot Act if they would take the time to actually read it.

Mukasey is attorney general of the United States. This viewpoint was excerpted from a speech he gave on his acceptance of the Learned Hand Medal for Excellence in Federal Jurisprudence, which appeared in full in the *Wall Street Journal*, May 10, 2004.

AS YOU READ, CONSIDER THE FOLLOWING QUESTIONS:

1. According to Mukasey, how many FBI agents are there world-wide?
2. How many subpoenas have been issued to librarians, according to the author?
3. According to the author, what did library records reveal in the investigation of the "Unabomber?"

L earned Hand, among the [twentieth] century's greatest judges, defined the spirit of liberty 60 years ago as "the spirit which is not too sure that it is right." We must consider what message we can take from those words today.

We are now in a struggle with an extremism that expresses itself in the form of terror attacks, and in that we face what is probably the gravest threat to this country's institutions, if not to its physical welfare, since the Civil War. When one tries to assess people who can find it in themselves to fly airplanes into buildings and murder 3,000 of us in a single morning, whatever else you can say about such people, they are very sure that they are right; and wouldn't it be music to their ears to hear that our spirit says we're not too sure that *we* are right?

Federal Investigations Are Legitimate

What measures we should take to protect ourselves, both abroad and at home, is now the subject of heated debate as we participate in a war against extremism, not so much to make the world safe for democracy as to achieve a more modest-sounding but, I would suggest, no less important goal—to make the world safe for us. Regrettably, like many debates, our current one already has seen its share of half-truths and outright falsehoods.

They began right after Sept. 11 [2001], when some claimed that FBI agents were rounding up Muslim Arabs wholesale and holding them incommunicado. That accusation seems dubious on its face when you consider that the FBI has only about 12,000 agents world-wide. That is not many when you realize that they investigate not only terrorism, but also every other federal crime aside from counterfeiting, tax evasion and mail fraud; that they share responsibility for drug investigations with the Drug Enforcement Administration—a pretty hefty set of assignments—and that they had numerous leads as to those responsible for the attack on Sept. 11. Under those circumstances—with many leads to work on and relatively few agents to do that work—does it really stand to reason that they spent their time rounding people up based on nothing other than religion and ethnicity?

No doubt there were people taken into custody, whether on immigration warrants or material witness warrants, who in retrospect should not have been. If those people have grievances redressable under the law, those grievances can be redressed. But we should keep in mind that any investigation conducted by fallible human beings in the aftermath of an attack is bound to be either overinclusive or underinclusive. There are consequences both ways. The consequences of overinclusiveness include condemnations. The consequences of underinclusiveness include condolences.

People Overreact to the Patriot Act

More recently, a statute called the USA Patriot Act has become the focus of a good deal of hysteria, some of it reflexive, much of it recreational.

My favorite example is the well-publicized resolution of the American Library Association condemning what the librarians claim to believe is a section of the statute that authorizes the FBI to obtain library records and to investigate people based on the books they take out. Some of the membership have announced a policy of destroying records so that they do not fall into the hands of the FBI.

United States attorney general Michael B. Mukasey argues that the current provisions of the Patriot Act provide a good balance between the rights of library patrons and the needs of law enforcement.

First a word on the organization that gives us this news. The motto of this organization is "Free people read freely." When it was called to their attention that there are 10 librarians languishing in Cuban prisons for encouraging their fellow countrymen to read freely, an imprisonment that has been condemned by [trade union leader and former president of Poland] Lech Walesa and [former president of Czechoslovakia and the Czech Republic] Vaclav Havel, among others, this association declined to vote any resolution of condemnation, although they did find time at their convention to condemn their own government. . . .

The Patriot Act Keeps Investigative Techniques Current

The provisions in the law that have generated the most opposition have to do with investigative techniques, including electronic surveillance and the gathering of business records. The electronic surveillance provisions give investigators access to cable-based communications, such as e-mail, on the same basis as they have long had access to telephone communications, and give them access to telephone communications in national security cases on the same basis on which they already have such access in drug cases.

I think most people would have been surprised and somewhat dismayed to learn that before the Patriot Act was passed, an FBI agent could apply to a court for a roving wiretap if a drug dealer switched cell phones, as they often do, but not if an identified agent of a foreign terrorist organization did; and could apply for a wiretap to investigate illegal sports betting, but not to investigate a potentially catastrophic computer hacking attack, the killing of U.S. nationals abroad, or the giving of material support to a terrorist organization. Violations like those simply were not on the list of offenses for which wiretaps could be authorized. . . .

Libraries Are Not Under Threat

What about the section the librarians were so concerned about, Section 215? Well, it bears some mention that the word *library* appears nowhere in that section. What the section does authorize is the issuance of subpoenas for tangible things, including business records, but only upon approval by the Foreign Intelligence Surveillance Court. Such a subpoena can direct everyone, including the record keeper, not to disclose the subpoena to anyone, including to the person whose records were obtained. That section also specifically forbids investigation of a citizen or a lawful alien solely on the basis of activity protected by the First Amendment. It requires that the Justice Department report to Congress every six months on subpoenas issued under it. At last report, there have been no such subpoenas issued to libraries. Indeed, there have been no such subpoenas, period.

Let me hasten to add that it is not impossible to imagine how library records might prove highly relevant, as they did in one case, very much pre-9/11—the case of the "Unabomber," Ted Kaczynski. Some of you may recall that Kaczynski was apprehended soon after a newspaper agreed to publish his manifesto, and was caught based principally on a tip from his brother, who read the manifesto, and recognized the rhetoric. But one of the ways that tip was proved accurate was through examination of library records, which disclosed that the three arcane books cited in the manifesto had been checked out to Ted Kaczynski from a local library—a devastating bit of corroborative circumstantial evidence.

It Helps to Read the Patriot Act

Like any other act of Congress, the Patriot Act should be scrutinized, criticized and, if necessary, amended. But in order to scrutinize and criticize it, it helps to read what is actually in it. It helps not to conduct the debate in terms that suggest it gives the government the power to investigate us based on what we read, or that people who work for the government actually have the inclination to do such a thing, not to mention the spare time.

As we participate in this debate on what is the right course to pursue, I think it is important to remember an interesting structural feature of the Constitution we all revere. When we speak of constitutional rights, we generally speak of rights that appear not in the original Constitution itself, but rather in amendments to the Constitution—principally the first 10. Those amendments are a noble work, but it is the rest of the Constitution—the boring part—the part that sets up a bicameral legislature and separation of powers, and so on, the part you will never see mentioned in any flyer or hear at any rally, that guarantees that the rights referred to in those 10 amendments are worth something more than the paper they are written on.

Have More Faith in the U.S. Government

A bill of rights was omitted from the original Constitution over the objections of Patrick Henry and others. It may well be that those who drafted the original Constitution understood that if you give equal prominence to the provisions creating the government and the provisions guaranteeing rights against the government—God-given rights, no less, according to the Declaration of Independence—then citizens will feel that much less inclined to sacrifice in behalf of their government, and that much more inclined simply to go where their rights and their interests seem to take them.

So, as the historian Walter Berns has argued, the built-in message —the hidden message in the structure of the Constitution—is that the government it establishes is entitled, at least in the first instance, to receive from its citizens the benefit of the doubt. If we keep that in mind, then the spirit of liberty will be the spirit which, if it is not too sure that it is right, is at least sure enough to keep itself—and us—alive.

Section 215 of the Patriot Act

Proponents of the Patriot Act argue that Section 215 does not violate Americans' library-use privacy. Furthermore, they assert that Section 215 is narrow in scope and cannot be used to gather intelligence on Americans or those who are legal residents.

- A FISA judge may grant an FBI request for an order that allows access to any relevant "tangible" item—including books, records, papers, documents, etc., but only in specific matters relating to terrorism investigations.
- Order must be used to gather foreign intelligence that does not concern an American.
- Order must be related to the U.S. ability to protect against attacks, sabotage, or spying from a foreign power or its agents.
- Order must relate to U.S. national security or threats of international terrorism.
- Order may be used to investigate an American only when, "any investigation of an American is not based solely on the American's exercise of his or her First Amendment rights."
- Those who receive the order may not disclose specifics included in the order.

EVALUATING THE AUTHOR'S ARGUMENTS:

The author of this viewpoint, Michael B. Mukasey, is the attorney general of the United States. The author of the previous viewpoint, Emily Drabinski, is a librarian. Does knowing the background of the authors influence your opinion of their arguments? In what way?

The Patriot Act Threatens Immigrants

Pittsburgh Bill of Rights Defense Campaign

"Fighting terrorism does not entail suspending the civil liberties of the people who created America— immigrants."

In the following viewpoint the authors argue that the constitutional rights of immigrants are violated under the Patriot Act. For example, the right to due process —the idea that the government must respect all of a person's rights as granted in the Fifth Amendment—is violated each time an immigrant is deported or detained for weeks on end. Furthermore, the authors say the Sixth Amendment is broken when, under the Patriot Act, immigrants are denied swift or public trials. In addition, the Patriot Act allows federal agents to make arrests for minor violations without having to reveal evidence against the detainee, which the authors say violates the probable cause doctrine. The authors point out that the government's abuse of power has been recognized and appears in a Department of Justice report. For these reasons, the authors conclude that the United States should be able to conduct

Pittsburgh Bill of Rights Defense Campaign (PBORDC), "Immigrants and the Patriot Act," 2005. Reproduced by permission.

its war on terror while maintaining democratic values and protecting immigrants' rights.

The Pittsburgh Bill of Rights Defense Campaign (PBORDC) educates people about potentially damaging effects of the USA PATRIOT Act on people's fundamental rights. PBORDC opposes any federal laws that infringe on civil liberties.

AS YOU READ, CONSIDER THE FOLLOWING QUESTIONS:

1. According to the authors what message about immigrants' rights was sent by the Supreme Court ruling in the case of *Zadvydas v. Davis*?
2. How many immigrants have been detained since 9/11, according to the authors?
3. How long do the authors say some immigrants have been detained while the FBI investigated their cases?

I ronically, the U.S.A. PATRIOT Act states "Arab Americans, Muslim Americans, and Americans from South Asia play a vital role in our Nation and are entitled to nothing less than the full rights of every American" (Sec. 102).

Immigrants' Rights Are Being Denied

Why is this so ironic, so hypocritical? Because in actuality this Act deliberately tramples the Bill of Rights by depriving immigrants and non-citizens the rights they are entitled to receive under the Constitution. How can America be so quick to judge and "reform" other nations into democratic ones, when we are not even preserving our own democracy by denying immigrants their rights?

"No person shall . . . be deprived of life, liberty, or property, without due process of law . . ." (5th Amendment)

In the 1896 Supreme Court ruling *Wong v. United States*, the Court held that the rights afforded to Americans also applied to immigrants and deportable non-citizens. In the 2001 case *Zadvydas v. Davis*, the

Supreme Court reaffirmed immigrants' rights and went so far as to say that Constitutional rights are guaranteed to all persons within U.S. boundaries, be they citizens or aliens. The PATRIOT Act, however, has thrown these precedents out the window in a blatant disregard for judicial oversight and disrespect for separation of powers.

Improper Detainment

One of the provisions of the act (Sec. 412) that erodes Constitutional rights allows for the immediate detention and deportation of immigrants who have merely been suspected of committing immigration violations. In other words, immigrants can be deported and/or indefinitely detained even if they have not been suspected of terrorist activity or committing a major crime. Even overstaying a tourist visa

Many opponents of the Patriot Act point to its disregard of immigrants' rights as evidence of its infringement on civil liberties.

by a single day could qualify their deportation. Before the PATRIOT Act, this minor violation would normally qualify the non-citizen to be released on bond. Detaining them clearly violates their right to equal protection implied under the due process clause.

Due process requirements warrant that immigrants can remain incarcerated only so long as their deportation issuance is pending. However, under the PATRIOT Act many detainees remained incarcerated weeks, and even months, after their deportation was issued. If their country of origin refuses to accept them, the Act allows immigrants to be detained indefinitely.

FAST FACT

Section 402 of the Patriot Act calls for hiring three times the number of Border Patrol, customs agents, and immigration inspectors along the U.S.-Canada border. It also allots $50 million each to customs and immigration to improve their monitoring technologies.

If an alien has been accused as a suspected terrorist or other threat to national security, he or she can be detained for up to 7 days without being charged for a crime, again a violation of the due process clause. The only requirement for someone to be certified as a terrorist under the PATRIOT Act is for the Attorney General to claim he has "reasonable grounds to believe" a non-citizen is involved in terrorist activities (Sec. 412). This vague and broad wording can be easily manipulated to satisfy the government's agenda to detain and interrogate anyone they choose.

No Speedy or Public Trials

"In all criminal prosecutions, the accused shall enjoy the right to a speedy and public trial . . ." (6th Amendment)

The PATRIOT Act does not entitle immigrants to a trial or hearing in which the government must prove the detainees' guilt, and according to Amnesty International, some detainees who requested that they be allowed to contact their attorneys to refute the accusations against them were refused.

The PATRIOT Act calls for minimal judicial oversight, meaning that the Attorney General and Department of Justice (DOJ) can arrest whomever they want without answering to anyone. They never have to reveal any of their supposed "evidence" against the detainees, which fails to satisfy the probable cause doctrine of the Constitution. In addition, this act does not require that the government must prove the detainee is guilty beyond all reasonable doubt, as is necessary in criminal trials, or present clear, convincing, and unequivocal evidence as used in deportation hearings. For the lucky detainees that do get a hearing, it may be done in complete secrecy and there have been instances in which the existence of such hearings has been denied altogether by the government.

Rounding Up Immigrants

Even scarier than knowing that the PATRIOT Act allows the government to detain people without giving them a public hearing or trial in which evidence against the detainees is presented, is that the government has not released the identities of all of the detainees. In the months following the 9/11 attacks, there were many reported cases of families having no idea where their loved ones had disappeared to, and even lawyers and human rights workers continue to find it impossible to make contact with immigrant detainees that were arrested under the PATRIOT Act.

Over 1,200 immigrants of mostly Arab and South Asian descent have been detained since September 11th; of these only one detainee has been charged with a crime related to September 11th and most of the other detainees are being held for common immigration paperwork violations. These minor violations clearly do not pose a threat to national security and have no bearing on what the PATRIOT Act proposes to do (to intercept and obstruct terrorism). The detentions, then, reveal the government's fear that any immigrant is a potential terrorist and it is best to suspend as many immigrants' rights as possible in the off-chance that one of them is a terrorist.

Ashcroft and the DOJ refuse to disclose basic information about many of the detainees, such as their names, the reasons for their arrests, and where they are being held. The Justice Department even announced that they would stop keeping count of how many people they were detaining! In August 2002, a federal judge declared that the detention of the immigrants was not warranted and the government had not provided any evidence that it has a standard by which

Americans Are Unclear About the Patriot Act

A 2006 poll found that although Americans have learned more about the Patriot Act in recent years, most of them are only "somewhat familiar" with the provisions of the act.

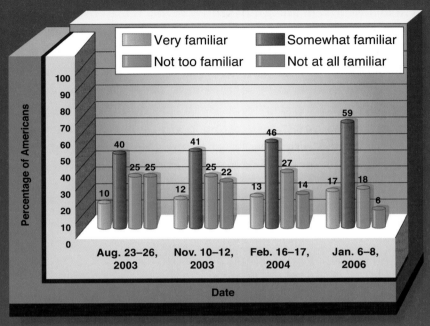

Taken from: *USA Today*/CNN Gallup Poll, January 6–8, 2006. www.usatoday.com/news/polls/2006-01-09-poll.htm.

it detains people. The judge ruled further that the government has violated the Freedom of Information Act by refusing to disclose basic information about detainees.

Detainees Are Being Abused

The government's overwhelming desire for secrecy has proved to open the door to human rights abuses against immigrants. There are numerous reports from various sources that detainees have been both physically and verbally abused, denied access to lawyers, food, medicines, forced to spend prolonged periods in solitary confinement, and forced to sleep standing up or on concrete floors in freezing conditions without blankets. A recently released Office of the

Inspector General (OIG) of the DOJ report further exposed the government's abuse of power. According to the report, detainees were not given "timely notification of the grounds for their detention" making it impossible to effectively defend themselves. In addition, the FBI held detainees until they were cleared of any wrongdoing, which often took more than ten weeks! These immigrants were also not given an opportunity to be released on bond and there was no distinction made between immigrants who were being held for terrorist activities and those who were being held for immigration violations.

Of course it is necessary to find and arrest those involved with terrorist activities. But is it necessary to abandon the democratic values embedded in our Constitution in doing so? If our democracy cannot stand up to terrorism by preserving our cherished freedoms, the terrorists have essentially succeeded in destroying our way of life. Fighting terrorism does not entail suspending the civil liberties of the people who created America—immigrants.

EVALUATING THE AUTHORS' ARGUMENTS:

In this viewpoint the authors argue that the U.S. government deprives immigrants of their constitutional rights. The authors of the next viewpoint, *Customs and Border Protection Today*, believe that the U.S. government protects the rights of immigrants. After reading both viewpoints, with which authors' perspective do you agree? Why?

The Patriot Act Does Not Threaten Law-Abiding Immigrants

Customs and Border Protection Today

"*Permanent resident aliens have a legal right to work, play, and move freely through our communities.*"

In the following viewpoint editors at *Customs and Border Protection Today* argue that because immigrants are the people most likely to harm the United States the Patriot Act must make restrictions on immigration, but it does not threaten the rights of law-abiding immigrants. The authors describe how the Patriot Act has helped law enforcement agencies track and manage 10 million legal immigrants living in the United States. For example, the act set up security systems and immigrant safeguards to help protect the United States from terror attacks. The authors argue that these systems are reasonable, and it is fair to ask immigrants to comply with them. The authors contend that when the permanent resident aliens, non-U.S. citizens, and foreign nationals visiting or studying in the United States follow the

Customs and Border Protection Today, "Immigration: The Gatekeepers," August 2003. www.cbp.gov/xp/CustomsToday/2003/august/ins_gatekeepers.xml.

required security measures, they are acting within the law, and thus their rights are preserved. The authors remind readers that although personal stories of immigrants dealing with immigration laws and policies may seem emotionally compelling, no immigrant rights have been violated. They conclude that it is more important to secure U.S. borders and keep Americans safe from future terrorist attacks than to avoid inconveniencing immigrants.

Customs and Border Protection Today, from which this viewpoint is taken, is the official employee newsletter of U.S. Customs and Border Protection and is published bimonthly.

AS YOU READ CONSIDER THE FOLLOWING QUESTIONS:

1. What fact about the 9/11 hijackers do the authors say jarred Americans out of their complacency about immigration?
2. How many undocumented immigrants live in the United States, according to the authors?
3. What is the US-VISIT program, as described by the authors?

Things will never be the same—the terrorist attacks of September 11 [2001] robbed us of our national innocence and changed the way we view our world. Mundane things and people, scarcely noticed before, are now transformed into objects meriting suspicion and scrutiny. Is that shopping bag sitting next to a trashcan a hiding place for a bomb or a chemical weapon? The foreign or unusually dressed man on the metro train is no longer an example of the richness and diversity of our society, but a potential terrorist.

These attacks also fueled public anxiety over the security of our borders. Jarred out of our complacency by the knowledge that some of the terrorists were foreign nationals living in this country illegally, Americans demanded to know: "Who's minding the store? Who is in the country? Where are they living? And what are they doing?"

The United States Needs Effective Immigration Laws

The United States—a cultural "melting pot" with a genuine commitment to diversity, human rights, and liberty. Who would not want to come? And people do come: as tourists, students and workers. Some are in pursuit of economic opportunity, and others are trying to escape tyranny or political persecution. They come for weeks, months, or years—some stay indefinitely. Some arrive illegally, risking their lives to cross our borders or using their life savings to pay for falsified entry documents.

Effective immigration laws and policies are meant to control and manage legal entry across our borders. For many years, America welcomed the majority of visitors with a smile and benign expectations. We were oceans away from the violence and terrorism that plagued Europe and the Mideast. Today, after 9/11, we have new expectations, and we are busily installing a host of new security systems to protect our homeland and the American people.

Fact and Fiction About the Patriot Act

The USA Patriot Act has been blamed for immigrant-related policies that are not actually included in its 342 pages.

The Patriot Act does/did *not*:

- Give the Justice Department power to detain hundreds of Middle Eastern men after the 9/11 attacks. (This was done under immigration laws.)

- Allow the government to hold 650 suspected Taliban and al-Qaeda operatives at the U.S. Naval Base at Guantanamo Bay, Cuba, as "enemy combatants" without access to lawyers of U.S. courts. (President George W. Bush imposed this policy based on his status as commander in chief during wartime.)

- Allow authorities to hold two U.S. citizens as "enemy combatants" at a Navy brig without charges or access to U.S. courts. (Bush imposed this policy, also based on his war powers under the Constitution.)

- Create military tribunals to try noncitizens who are accused of terrorism offenses. (Bush authorized the tribunals in November 2001.)

- Allow FBI agents to enter houses of worship or attend political rallies while investigating terrorism. (Former attorney general John Ashcroft made this possible by changing Justice Department rules for investigators.)

Taken from: Toni Locy, "Patriot Act Blurred in the Public Mind," *USA Today*, February 25, 2004. wwwusatoday.com/tech/news/techpolicy/2004-02-25-patriot-main_x.htm.

Permanent Resident Aliens Have Legal Rights

The green card, as everyone calls it, is an important alien registration security mechanism. This Permanent Legal-Resident Card lets authorities know that permanent resident aliens have a legal right to work, play, and move freely through our communities. Nonimmigrant aliens, people authorized to be in the country for temporary periods, must always carry a valid passport and an Arrival-Departure Record (I-94). Then, of course, there is the "sweetheart visa" (K-1), that critical little piece of paper Uncle Sam insists that a foreign bride or groom must have to be able to tie the knot.

Last year [2002], the Justice Department also announced that all non–U.S. citizens were required to provide notice to immigration officials of changes in their U.S. address within 10 days of any move. The requirement is not new and is based on a law that has been in place for over 50 years. Previously, the risk was not thought sufficient to warrant the resources necessary to stringently enforce the law, which applies to 10 million people living in the United States legally as well as to 8 or 9 million undocumented immigrants.

Foreign Students Comply with New Security Measures

One of the ironies surrounding 9/11 was the fact that several of the terrorists who engineered the attack had entered the country on student visas. They obtained the skills and expertise they needed to launch their assault right here in American schools. The USA Patriot Act, passed on October 26, 2001, provided law enforcement agencies with the tools they needed to identify, expel, and prevent terrorists from entering the country. Most importantly, the Patriot Act allows for tighter controls on foreign students.

In the past, foreign nationals who wanted to study in this country could enter the country under student provisions without having

> **FAST FACT**
>
> In 2005 anti-money-laundering provisions in the Patriot Act allowed the United States Customs and Immigration Enforcement to report the arrests of more than 155 people, 142 criminal indictments, and seizure of more than $25 million in illegal profits.

At a news conference in 2002, then attorney general John Ashcroft (right) announces the creation of the National Security Entry-Exit Registration System. The system was designed to register and track visitors to the United States who may pose a threat to national security.

made application to any school. No more. Today foreign students need a letter of admission from an American school before they can enter the country. Another security measure: foreign nationals in the country under different provisions can request a change to student status, but they cannot begin their studies until they receive student status approval. Before the Patriot Act, they could start studying in the United States while waiting for approval.

On May 10, 2002, the Attorney General announced the Student and Exchange Visitor Information System (SEVIS) regulations. SEVIS is the next step in tracking and monitoring technology of non-immigrant students, exchange visitors, and their dependents. Implementation of an interactive portion of the system began on a voluntary basis on July 1, 2002, but on August 1, 2003, schools who have enrolled foreign students are now required to participate in SEVIS.

SEVIS captures vital information, such as the address of the student, port of entry, date of entry, and visa information. In addition, the course of study, record of enrollment, and courses completed must be entered—detailed academic information that provides evidence that non-resident students are really here to study.

Foreign Visitors Comply with a New Registration System

The Patriot Act requires that DHS [Department of Homeland Security] develop an entry-exit system that will provide greater protection for the United States and help aliens fulfill their responsibilities under U.S. law. NSEER [National Security Entry-Exit Registration System], also known as "special registration," translates into a simple mandate: visiting foreign nationals identified as high-risk must be fingerprinted at the port of entry and matched against a database of known criminals and terrorists. These visitors are selected on the basis of intelligence criteria that reflect patterns of terrorist activity. Periodically, foreign visitors here for more than 30 days or annually are required to register to confirm their place of residence and the reason for their continued presence in the U.S.

There is another change as well—instead of leaving the country at their own discretion, foreign visitors must leave from designated ports of entry where they are required to "check-out" and provide the details of their departure. This way immigration officials know immediately when a high-risk alien overstays his visa.

By the end of 2003, the US-VISIT [United States Visitor and Immigrant Status Indication Technology] system will have replaced the special registration program. It will incorporate the SEVIS system and meet the congressional requirements for an automated entry-exit system. US-VISIT will use biometric identifiers, such as photographs and fingerprints, to track and monitor visitors. DHS Secretary Tom Ridge characterized US-VISIT as an "electronic check-in/check-out system for people who come to the United States to work or to study or visit."

Our First Priority Should Be Security

Media coverage of heart-rending stories of immigrants caught up in a tangle of law and regulations are everywhere. Each has mitigating and complicating factors—children whose parents face deportation, men without terrorist ties who came forward to register only to be told they were here illegally. Every story is different, and each one illustrates the complexities that attend this issue. However, when it comes to protecting our homeland, it's not complicated at all. Our first priority is to secure our borders.

EVALUATING THE AUTHORS' ARGUMENTS:

In this viewpoint the authors suggest that after the 9/11 terrorist attacks, the best thing that the United States can do is to enhance security measures that manage and control the legal entry of millions of immigrants across the U.S. borders. How do you think each of the other authors in this chapter might respond to this suggestion? List each author and write two to three sentences on what you think their response might be.

Journalists Are Threatened by the Patriot Act

"Journalists should be concerned about certain provisions of the law, which . . . make previous statutory protections for newsrooms almost irrelevant when it comes to terrorism investigations."

Reporters Committee for Freedom of the Press

In the following viewpoint the author argues that the Patriot Act gives the U.S. government expansive surveillance powers that hinder journalists' ability to report on the war on terror. The author explains that under the Patriot Act the FBI is able to confiscate reporters' notes and confidential sources during a terrorism investigation. If a reporter contacts someone who is proven to be the target of a foreign intelligence investigation, there is a Patriot Act provision that allows the FBI to wiretap the phone or e-mail communications of the journalist. In the past, journalists have had the freedom to report on government activities and maintain the confidentiality of their sources, but the author warns that the Patriot Act threatens this important independence. Because the freedom of the press is vital to the political health of the country, the author argues that the Patriot Act should not infringe on reporters' rights.

The Reporters Committee for Freedom of the Press is a group of volunteer attorneys who provide free legal assistance to journalists who find themselves with First Amendment and freedom of information problems.

AS YOU READ, CONSIDER THE FOLLOWING QUESTIONS:
1. What does the phrase "tangible things" mean in the context of this viewpoint?
2. What has the Patriot Act made it easier for investigators to do to journalists' phone calls and e-mails, according to the author?
3. Who is John Solomon, and how does he figure into the author's argument?

The USA PATRIOT Act's impact on newsgathering is still largely theoretical nearly four years after Congress rushed to enact the law. No newsrooms are known to have been searched and apparently no documents have been taken from reporters under the law—although those subject to such a search and seizure would be prohibited from talking about it.

U.S. Surveillance Powers Are Expanded Under the Patriot Act

Nevertheless, journalists should be concerned about certain provisions of the law, which grant broad new powers to government agents to investigate terrorism and make previous statutory protections for newsrooms almost irrelevant when it comes to terrorism investigations.

Congress enacted the law with little debate just six weeks after the terrorist attacks on the World Trade Center and the Pentagon. President Bush signed the USA PATRIOT Act into law on Oct. 26, 2001.

The awkwardly named law—the Uniting and Strengthening America by Providing Appropriate Tools Required to Intercept and Obstruct Terrorism Act of 2001—expands the FBI's ability to obtain records through secret court orders. The law also gives government investigators greater authority to track e-mail and telephone communications and to eavesdrop on those conversations.

Although aimed at trapping terrorists, those provisions of the law could ensnare journalists and compromise their ability to report on the war on terrorism. Journalists should be aware of this law and future amendments and proposals that attempt to expand government surveillance powers and increase secrecy surrounding the government's efforts to combat terrorism. . . .

Newsrooms Can Be Searched During a Terrorism Investigation

Under Section 215 of the PATRIOT Act, the FBI can seek an order requiring the production of "any tangible thing"—which the law says includes books, records, papers, documents and other items—from anyone for investigations involving foreign intelligence or international terrorism. The person or business receiving the order cannot tell anyone that the FBI sought or obtained the "tangible things."

For journalists, the big question is whether the provision for secret court orders will allow a newsroom search for "any tangible thing" related to a terrorism investigation. Could a government agent use the law to gain access to a reporter's notes and confidential sources?

The short answer is that the PATRIOT Act does allow the search of newsrooms in connection with terrorism investigations. Another federal law, the Privacy Protection Act of 1980, spells out when newsroom searches are forbidden and the limited exceptions in which they are allowed. However, it only applies to criminal investigations, and the FBI has made it clear that the PATRIOT Act's application to any "investigation to protect against international terrorism or clandestine intelligence activities" does not subject it to the limits of criminal investigations.

Journalists Need to Protect Their Work

The Privacy Protection Act states that, "notwithstanding any other law," federal and state officers and employees are prohibited from searching or seizing a journalist's "work product" or "documentary materials" in the journalist's possession, as part of a criminal investigation. A journalist's work product includes notes and drafts of news

The Patriot Act Has Been Abused

According to the Office of the Inspector General, between 2004 and 2005 a percentage of various kinds of communications were inappropriately accessed by the FBI. Some of these communications were accessed in violation of the law. Some were outside the scope of the law, while others were unauthorized.

Category	2004	2005
ELSUR (Electronic Surveillance) not within authorized time period		
· Telephone communications/audio recordings	3.2%	2.2%
· Facsimile number intercept	3.2%	0.0%
· E-mail communication	4.8%	4.4%
ELSUR Not Within Authorized Time Period Subtotal	**11.2%**	**6.6%**
ELSUR outside scope/intent of FISC (Foreign Intelligence Surveillance Court) order		
· Incorrect telephone number	9.5%	8.9%
· Telephone communications/audio recordings	12.7%	11.1%
· Incorrect facsimile number	0.0%	4.4%
· Facsimile intercept	0.0%	4.4%
· Incorrect e-mail address	3.2%	6.7%
· E-mail communication	4.8%	15.6%
· Incorrect subject	4.8%	13.3%
· Other	9.5%	4.4%
Failure to comply with OIPR (Office of Intelligence Policy and Review) directive to terminate collection	**3.2%**	**0%**
ELSUR Not Authorized by FISC Order Subtotal	**47.7%**	**68.8%**
· Improper use of ELSUR to access financial and other records	3.2%	2.2%
· FISA (Foreign Intelligence Surveillance Act) physical search conducted prior to receipt of Emergency Authorization from the Attorney General	3.2%	0.0%
· Unauthorized or improper dissemination	3.2%	0.0%
· Violation of minimization procedures	3.2%	0.0%
AG (Attorney General) Guidelines/FBI Policy Subtotal	**39.7%**	**53.3%**

Taken from: Office of the Inspector General analysis of files provided by FBI-OGC (Office of General Counsel).

stories. Documentary materials include videotapes, audiotapes and computer disks.

Some limited exceptions under the Privacy Protection Act allow the government to search for or seize certain types of national security information, child pornography, evidence that a journalist has committed a crime, or documentary materials that must be immediately seized to prevent death or serious bodily injury.

Documentary materials also may be seized under the Privacy Protection Act if there is reason to believe that they would be destroyed in the time it took government officers to seek a subpoena. Those materials also can be seized if a court has ordered disclosure, the news organization has refused and all other remedies have been exhausted.

Under Section 215 of the Patriot Act, the FBI can require newsrooms to produce any "tangible thing" that relates to investigations on terrorism, which makes it difficult for reporters to maintain their sources' confidentiality.

The Privacy Protection Act gives journalists the right to sue the United States or a state government, or federal and state employees, for damages for violating the law. The law also allows journalists to recover attorney's fees and court costs. . . .

The Press's Rights Are Challenged by the Patriot Act

As long as a reporter is not an "agent of a foreign power," the PATRIOT Act does not make it easier for the government to wiretap a reporter's phone. As was the case before the law passed, investigators still must have probable cause to believe a person has committed a crime before they can bug that person's phone.

However, it is now easier for investigators to eavesdrop on a terrorism suspect's telephone calls and e-mail communications with so-called "roving" wiretaps. Because of that change, reporters may run a heightened risk of having their telephone or e-mail conversations with sources intercepted by government agents if those sources are deemed "agents of a foreign power."

FAST FACT

Section 216 of the Patriot Act allows pen register and trap-and-trace devices to be installed on phones, Internet, and e-mail accounts in order to gather dialing, routing, addressing, and signaling information.

Though these legislative initiatives do not directly address journalists, any rollback in protection of private communications can affect reporters' relations with sources. Furthermore, these actions provide insight on where the future of antiterrorism law may lead—a road that may pose grave danger to the First Amendment rights of the press.

Journalists should become familiar with the electronic surveillance features of the new law because those provisions pose a potential threat to newsgathering. . . .

Secret Surveillance

As was the case before the PATRIOT Act passed, government investigators cannot wiretap a reporter's phones and e-mail accounts unless they had probable cause that the reporter had committed or was about to commit a crime.

But by contacting someone who is the target of foreign intelligence surveillance, the reporter might be vulnerable to having a pen register or trap-and-trace device placed on the reporter's phone and e-mail accounts, because the government agent has to certify to a secret court only that the information likely to be obtained would be relevant to an ongoing foreign intelligence investigation. Once approved, the devices give investigators a list of every e-mail address and phone number the reporter is contacting, although not the contents of those communications.

And because all of this goes on in secret, the reporter may never know that his or her communications have been under government surveillance.

How likely is this to happen? No one knows. In their June 2002 letter to Ashcroft seeking information on how the Justice Department was implementing the PATRIOT Act, Reps. [F. James] Sensenbrenner [Jr.] and [John] Conyers [Jr.] of the House Judiciary Committee asked how many times the department had obtained permission for roving wiretaps, pen registers and trap-and-trace devices. The congressmen did not ask how many times journalists had been caught up in such investigations.

[Daniel J.] Bryant, the assistant attorney general who responded to the letter, did not provide the information to Sensenbrenner and Conyers. Instead, he wrote them that the information on roving wiretaps was classified; he did not respond at all to the question on pen registers and trap-and-trace devices.

Patriot Act Guidelines Are Ignored

Reporters do have a measure of protection in the Attorney General's Guidelines for Subpoenaing Members of the News Media, which have been in place since the Nixon Administration. Those guidelines, which do not carry the force of law, require that news media subpoenas identify particular relevant information that cannot be obtained any other way. The guidelines also call for negotiations between the Justice Department and the reporter when the agency seeks a subpoena against the news media (28 C.F.R. § 50.10).

The Bush administration has shown that it will ignore those guidelines if it believes the reporter might have information that could help a criminal investigation.

The Justice Department violated the guidelines in 2001 when it subpoenaed the telephone records of Associated Press reporter John Solomon. The agency was trying to discover the reporter's confidential source for information about a now-closed investigation of Sen. Robert Torricelli (D-N.J.).

Solomon did not learn until late August 2001 about the subpoena, which covered his phone records from May 2 to 7, 2001. The Justice Department did not negotiate with Solomon or his employer, did not say why the reporter's phone records were essential to a criminal investigation, and did not explain why the information could not be obtained any other way.

Also, the Justice Department ignored a provision in the guidelines that allows no more than a 90-day delay in notifying a reporter about a subpoena. The department missed that deadline in the Solomon case.

The Solomon subpoena was issued before September 11 and before Congress enacted the PATRIOT Act. But it could be a bellwether event in gauging the willingness of the Bush administration to use journalists as a tool of surveillance—with the PATRIOT-aided twist of no longer notifying journalists when they are implicated in these investigations.

EVALUATING THE AUTHOR'S ARGUMENTS:

In the viewpoint you just read, the author uses history, facts, and examples to show how journalists' privacy rights are violated and how work products may be seized during terrorism investigations under the Patriot Act. The author does not use quotations, however, to support this point. If you were to rewrite this article and insert quotations, what authorities might you quote from? Where would you place these quotations to bolster the points this author makes?

Facts About the Patriot Act

Editor's note: These facts can be used in reports or papers to reinforce or add credibility when making important points or claims.

The Patriot Act's Conception and History

- The USA PATRIOT Act of 2001 stands for *U*niting and *S*trengthening *A*merica by *P*roviding *A*ppropriate *T*ools *Re*quired to *I*ntercept and *O*bstruct *T*errorism.
- On October 11, 2001, the act passed 98 votes to 1 in the U.S. Senate. Democratic senator Russell Feingold from Wisconsin cast the only dissenting vote.
- On October 12, 2001, the House of Representatives voted 357–66 to pass the act.
- The USA Patriot Act was signed into law by President George W. Bush on October 26, 2001—forty-five days after the September 11 terrorist attacks.
- On March 2, 2006, the U.S. Senate voted 89–10 to renew the USA Patriot Act. Democratic senator Daniel Inouye from Hawaii did not cast a vote.
- On March 7, 2006, the House renewed the Patriot Act 280-138. Eleven Democrats and three Republicans did not cast their votes.
- On March 9, 2006, President Bush signed the USA PATRIOT Improvement and Reauthorization Act.

The USA PATRIOT Improvement and Reauthorization Act

- Includes the Combat Methamphetamine Epidemic Act of 2005. This bill makes several ingredients used to manufacture methamphetamine more difficult to buy.
- Creates a new position for an assistant attorney general for national security. This provision permits the Justice Depart-

ment to bring its intelligence surveillance operations under one authority.

- Creates a new sunset of December 31, 2009, for USA PATRIOT Act sections 206 and 215 (roving wiretaps).
- Provides for greater congressional and judicial oversight of sections 206 and 215.
- Requires high-level approval to access records related to section 215 Foreign Intelligence Surveillance Act (FISA) orders that involve libraries, bookstores, gun sales, medical records, tax returns, and educational records.
- Gives more oversight concerning "sneak-and-peek" search warrants.
- Expands the list for acceptable wiretap orders to include more than twenty federal crimes.

The reauthorization made permanent the following sections that were set to expire:

- 201. Wiretapping used during terrorism investigations.
- 202. Wiretapping in computer fraud and abuse cases.
- 203 (b)(d). Authority to share criminal investigative information.
- 204. Technical exception for foreign intelligence gathering.
- 207. Duration of FISA surveillance of non–United States citizens who are agents of a foreign power.
- 209. Seizure of voicemail pursuant to warrants.
- 212. Emergency disclosure of electronic communications to authorities without warrant or consumer consent.
- 214. Pen register and trap-and-trace authority under FISA with modifications by the Senate, requiring service providers to give investigators information about customers that is related to the investigation.
- 217. Interception of computer trespasser communications.
- 218. Lowers the standard of evidence required to issue FISA warrants when gathering foreign intelligence.
- 220. Nationwide service of search warrants for electronic evidence.
- 223. Civil liability and punishment for certain Electronic Communications Privacy Act (ECPA) or FISA violations.

- 225. Immunity for compliance with FISA wiretaps.
- 6603. Of the Intelligence Reform and Terrorism Prevention Act—this expands federal punishments to those who provide material support to terrorists.

American Opinions of the Patriot Act

A January 2006 poll conducted by CNN, *USA Today*, and Gallup found that:

- 50 percent of Americans agreed it was fine to forgo warrants when ordering surveillance of those suspected of having terrorist ties.
- 46 percent disagreed.
- 4 percent had no opinion.
- 75 percent of those polled said they had been following the issue of bypassing the special court when ordering wiretaps very closely or somewhat closely.
- 29 percent said the issue was, "extremely important" during the 2006 elections.
- 55 percent of participants stated that terrorism was an "extremely important" issue.
- 38 percent said that the Bush administration had restricted civil liberties too much.
- 40 percent believed that the administration's approach was "about right."
- 19 percent said the administration had not done enough.
- 13 percent said the Patriot Act should not be changed in any way.
- 50 percent said minor changes to the law were called for.
- 24 percent said major changes were in order.
- 7 percent said the Patriot Act should be repealed.

An October 2006 poll conducted by *USA Today* and Gallup found:

- 47 percent would disapprove of the repeal of the Patriot Act.
- 43 percent would approve the repeal of the Patriot Act.
- 11 percent had no opinion.

A survey conducted in January 2006 by the Pew Research Center discovered:

- 53 percent of Democrats believe that the Patriot Act threatens civil liberties.
- 25 percent of Democrats consider the Patriot Act necessary to help the government find terrorists.
- 39 percent of the public as a whole said the Patriot Act is necessary.
- 38 percent of the public as a whole said it threatens civil liberties.

Organizations to Contact

The editors have compiled the following list of organizations concerned with the issues debated in this book. The descriptions are derived from materials provided by the organizations. All have publications or information available for interested readers. The list was compiled on the date of publication of the present volume; the information provided here may change. Be aware that many organizations take several weeks or longer to respond to inquiries, so allow as much time as possible.

American Civil Liberties Union (ACLU)
125 Broad St., 18th Flr.
New York, NY 10004-2400
(212) 549-2500
e-mail: aclu@aclu.org
Web site: www.aclu.org

The American Civil Liberties Union is a national organization that works to defend the civil rights guaranteed by the U.S. Constitution, arguing that measures to protect national security should not compromise fundamental civil liberties. It has protested the Patriot Act in a variety of publications, Web pages, and public appearances and speeches.

American Enterprise Institute (AEI)
1150 Seventeenth St. NW
Washington, DC 20036
(202) 862-5800
Web site: www.aei.org

The American Enterprise Institute for Public Policy Research is a scholarly research institute that is dedicated to preserving limited government, private enterprise, and a strong foreign policy and national defense. It has produced several white papers relating to the Patriot Act.

Canadian Association for Free Expression (CAFE)
PO Box 332 Station 'B'
Etobicoke, ON M9W 5L3, CANADA
(905) 897-7221
e-mail: cafe@canadafirst.net
Web site: www.canadianfreespeech.com

CAFE, one of Canada's leading civil liberties groups, works to strengthen the freedom of speech and freedom of expression provisions in the Canadian Charter of Rights and Freedoms. It lobbies politicians and researches threats to freedom of speech. Publications related to the Patriot Act include specialized reports, leaflets, and the *Free Speech Monitor*, which is published ten times per year.

Cato Institute
1000 Massachusetts Ave. NW
Washington, DC 2001-5403
(202) 842-0200
e-mail: cato@cato.org
Web site: www.cato.org

The institute is a nonpartisan public policy research foundation dedicated to limiting the role of government and protecting individual liberties. Many of its reports and white papers have focused on the Patriot Act.

Center for Immigration Studies
1522 K St. NW, Ste. 820
Washington, DC 20005-1202
(202) 466-8185
e-mail: center@cis.org
Web site: www.cis.org

The Center for Immigration Studies is the nation's only think tank dedicated to research and analysis of the economic, social, and demographic impacts of immigration on the United States. The center supports a pro-immigrant and low-immigration policy. Available on the Web site are a number of publications, congressional testimonies, and panel discussion transcripts.

Center for Responsive Politics (CRP)
1101 Fourteenth St. NW, Ste. 1030
Washington, DC 20005-5635
(202) 857-0044 • fax: (202) 857-7809
e-mail: info@crp.org
Web site: www.opensecrets.org

The Center for Responsive Politics is a nonpartisan, nonprofit research group that tracks money in politics and its effect on elections, public policy, and democracy. The center's work is aimed at creating a more educated voter, an involved citizenry, and a more responsive government. It publishes the *Captial Eye* newsletter and numerous reports.

The Century Foundation
41 E. Seventieth St.
New York, NY 10021
(212) 535-4441 • fax: (212) 879-9197
e-mail: info@tcf.org
Web site: www.tcf.org

This research foundation, formerly known as the Twentieth Century Fund, sponsors analyses of economic policy, foreign affairs, and domestic political issues. It publishes numerous books, reports, and articles, many of which focus on the Patriot Act. It also hosts project sites, including Liberty Under Attack.org and Reform Elections.org.

Council on American-Islamic Relations (CAIR)
453 New Jersey Ave. SE
Washington, DC 20003
(202) 488-8787
e-mail: cair@cair-net.org
Web site: www.cair-net.org

CAIR is a nonprofit organization that challenges stereotypes of Islam and Muslims and offers an Islamic perspective on public policy issues. Several of its publications explore the effect the Patriot Act has had on Muslim and Arab Americans and immigrants.

Electronic Foundation (EFF)
454 Shotwell St.
San Francisco, CA 94110
(415) 436-9333
e-mail: eff@eff.org
Web site: www.eff.org

EFF is a watchdog organization for the preservation of civil liberties on the Internet. It develops positions on free speech, encryption, privacy, and intellectual property. The Web site offers information resources about the issues and links to legal cases and the organizations' white papers.

Electronic Privacy Information Center (EPIC)
1718 Connecticut Ave. NW, Ste. 200
Washington, DC 20009
(202) 483-1140
Web site: http://epic.org

EPIC was established in 1994 to focus public attention on emerging civil liberties issues and to protect privacy, the First Amendment, and constitutional values. The center has published a number of books about the law and citizens' involvement with the law, including *Beyond Fear: Thinking Sensibly About Security in an Uncertain World.*

Federal Bureau of Investigation (FBI)
935 Pennsylvania Ave. NW, Rm. 7972
Washington, DC 20535
(202) 324-3000
Web site: www.fbi.gov

The FBI, the principal investigative arm of the U.S. Department of Justice, has the authority and responsibility to investigate specific crimes assigned to it. The FBI also is authorized to provide other law enforcement agencies with cooperative services, such as fingerprint identification, laboratory examinations, and police training. The Web site has a special Records and Information section for students and other researchers where one can investigate the FBI and its work.

Federation of American Scientists (FAS)
1717 K St. NW, Ste. 209
Washington, DC 20036
(202) 546-3300
Web site: www.fas.org

The Federation of American Scientists was formed in 1945 by atomic scientists from the Manhattan Project who felt that scientists, engineers, and other innovators had an ethical obligation to bring their knowledge and experience to bear on critical national decisions, especially pertaining to the technology they unleashed—the atomic bomb. The FAS now publishes reports on many issues of national and political significance, including the Patriot Act.

Freedom Forum
1101 Wilson Blvd.
Arlington, VA 22209
(703) 528-0800 • fax: (703) 284-2836
e-mail: news@freedomforum.org
Web site: www.freedomforum.org

The Freedom Forum is an international organization that works to protect freedom of the press and free speech. It monitors developments in media and First Amendment issues on its Web site, in its monthly magazine *Forum News,* and in the *Media Studies Journal,* published twice a year.

People for the American Way (PFAW)
2000 M St. NW, Ste. 400
Washington, DC 20036
(202) 467-4999 or 1-800-326-PFAW • fax: (202) 293-2672
e-mail: pfaw@pfaw.org
Web site: www.pfaw.org

PFAW works to promote citizen participation in democracy and to safeguard the principles of the U.S. Constitution, including the right to free speech. It publishes a variety of fact sheets, articles, and position statements on its Web site and distributes the e-mail newsletter *Freedom to Learn Online.*

United States Department of Justice (DOJ)
950 Pennsylvania Ave. NW
Washington, DC 20530-0001
(202) 514-2000
e-mail: askdoj@usdoj.gov
Web site: www.usdoj.gov

The function of the DOJ is to enforce the law and defend the interests of the United States according to the law, to ensure public safety against foreign and domestic threats, to provide federal leadership in preventing and controlling crime, to seek just punishment for those guilty of unlawful behavior, to administer and enforce the nation's immigration laws fairly and effectively, and to ensure fair and impartial administration of justice for all Americans. Up-to-date announcements and news are available on the Web site.

Books

Brasch, Walter M. *America's Unpatriotic Acts: The Federal Government's Violation Of Constitutional and Civil Rights*. New York: Peter Lang, 2005. Looks not just at the effects of the Patriot Act upon the nation but also at the innumerable civil rights violations conducted in the United States, as well as by the United States in foreign countries, during the years following September 11, 2001, events.

Etzioni, Amitai. *How Patriotic Is the Patriot Act? Freedom Versus Security in an Age of Terrorism*. New York: Routledge, 2004. Assesses a variety of national security measures, arguing whether or not each measure is justified.

Finan, Chris. *From the Palmer Raids to the Patriot Act: A History of the Fight for Free Speech in America*. Boston: Beacon, 2008. Provides an insightful history of the long struggle for free speech in America, up to and including the effect the Patriot Act has had on free speech and democracy.

Greenwald, Glenn. *How Would a Patriot Act? Defending American Values from a President Run Amok*. San Francisco: Working Assets, 2006. One man's story of being galvanized into action to defend America's founding principles and a reasoned argument for what must be done.

Ibbetson, Paul A. *Living Under the Patriot Act: Educating a Society*. Bloomington, IN: AuthorHouse, 2007. A former police chief shares three years of research on what he calls "one of the most powerful laws of modern day."

Leone, Richard C., and Greg Anrig Jr., eds. *The War on Our Freedoms: Civil Liberties in an Age of Terrorism*. New York: Public Affairs, 2003. Features thirteen essays on civil liberties in the war on terrorism, most of which emphasize the need for checks and balances to prevent the abuse of counterterrorism measures.

Wong, Kam C. *The Impact of USA Patriot Act on American Society: An Evidence Based Assessment*. New York: Nova Science, 2007.

Offers scholarly research on the legislation, implementation, and impact of the Patriot Act.

Periodicals

Abourezk, James G. "Another 'Surge' Is Needed—This Time, of Common Sense," *Washington Report on Middle East Affairs*, vol. 27, no. 1, January/February 2008.

Anderson, Thomas. "Patriot Act Protects Americans from Terrorism," Discovery Institute, August 3, 2004. www.discovery.org/scripts/viewDB/index.php?command=view&id=2153.

Benoit, Mary. "Slipping Through Legislation: All Too Often Members of Congress Use Legislative Strategies to Secure the Passage of Harmful Bills That Would Otherwise Potentially Fail on the Congressional Floor," *New American*, October 1, 2007.

Berlau, John. "Making a Meth of the PATRIOT Act," *Reason*, February 23, 2006. www.reason.com/news/show/117336.html.

Bollag, Burton. "Scholars Kept Out," *Chronicle of Higher Education*, vol. 53, no. 41, June 15, 2007.

Bush, George W. "President Discusses Patriot Act," Ohio State Highway Patrol Academy, Columbus, Ohio, June 9, 2005. www.whitehouse.gov/news/releases/2005/06/20050609-2.html.

Clark, Wesley. "War Didn't and Doesn't Bring Democracy," *Washington Monthly*, May 2005.

Colson, Nicole. "Big Brother Is Watching You," *Socialist Worker*, January 27, 2006. www.socialistworker.org/2006-1/573/573_08_BigBrother.shtml.

Cusimano, Maryann. "Broken Promises: 'Refugees Are Being Stripped of Protection Due Them by Law,'" *America*, May 14, 2007.

Dinh, Viet D. "How the USA Patriot Act Defends Democracy," Foundation for the Defense of Democracies, June 1, 2004. www.defenddemocracy.org/usr_doc/USA_Patriot_Act_2.pdf.

Economist. "Learning to Live with Big Brother; Civil Liberties: Surveillance and Privacy," September 29, 2007.

Feingold, Russ. "Patriot Act Games," *Salon.com*, February 15, 2006. www.salon.com/opinion/feature/2006/02/15/traitors.

Fisher, William. "In Terror War, Not All Names Are Equal," Common Dreams.org, April 20, 2006. www.commondreams.org/head lines06/0420-06.htm.

Gause, F. Gregory. "Can Democracy Stop Terrorism?" *Foreign Affairs*, September/October, 2005. www.foreignaffairs. org/20050901faessay84506/f-gregory-gause-iii/can-democracy-stop-terrorism.html.

Holt, Pat M. "To Spread Democracy Abroad, Respect the Law at Home," *Christian Science Monitor*, February 2, 2006. www.cs monitor.com/2006/0202/p09s01-coop.html.

Humphrey, Michael. "Remember Privacy?" *National Catholic Reporter*, vol. 44, no. 2, November 2, 2007.

Mac Donald, Heather. "Patriot Act: Let Investigators Do Their Job," National Public Radio, July 20, 2005. www.npr.org/templates /story/story.php?storyId=4763326.

Madsen, Wayne. "Homeland Security, Homeland Profits," *Corp-Watch*, December 21, 2001. www.corpwatch.org/article.php?id= 1108.

Nation, "American Patriots," vol. 283, no. 3, July 17, 2006.

Olsen, Ken. "Patriot Act's Wide Net," *Nation*, vol. 285, no. 8, September 24, 2007.

Packer, George. "Keep Out," *New Yorker*, vol. 82, no. 33, October 16, 2006.

Paye, Jean-Claude. "A Permanent State of Emergency," *Monthly Review: An Independent Socialist Magazine*, vol. 58, no. 6, November 2006.

Pike, George H. "The PATRIOT Act Illuminated," *Information Today*, May 2007.

Sorcher, Alan E. "USA Patriot Act: Five Years and Counting, but Still More Work to Be Done," *Journal of Investment Compliance*, Winter 2006.

Thibault, Jon. "Patriot Act 101," *FrontPage Magazine.com*, April 1, 2004.

Tigar, Michael E. "The Twilight of Personal Liberty," *Monthly Review: An Independent Socialist Magazine*, vol. 58, no. 6, November 2006.

Zaal, Mayida, Tahani Salah, and Michelle Fine, "The Weight of the Hyphen: Freedom, Fusion and Responsibility Embodied by Young

Muslim-American Women During a Time of Surveillance," *Applied Developmental Science*, vol. 11, no. 3, 2007.

Web Sites

Department of Homeland Security (DHS) (www.dhs.gov). Offers a wide variety of information on homeland security, including press releases, speeches and testimony, and reports on new initiatives in the war on terrorism.

Electronic Privacy Information Center's Patriot Act Page (http://epic.org/privacy/terrorism/usapatriot). Contains news, information, overviews, and analyses of the USA Patriot Act, including many links to other helpful resources.

National Immigration Forum (NIF) (www.immigrationforum.org). Advocates public policies that welcome immigrants and refugees and that are fair and supportive to newcomers to the United States. The NIF Web site offers a special section on immigration in the wake of September 11, 2001.

Patriot Act—Free, Searchable, Online (www.asksam.com/eBooks /Patriot_Act). This Web site provides a complete up-to-date searchable copy of the Patriot Act that is available online or downloaded to a computer.

Preserving Life and Liberty (www.lifeandliberty.gov). Set up by the U.S. Department of Justice to address civil libertarians' concerns about the Patriot Act and other homeland security initiatives. Offers answers to frequently asked questions about the Patriot Act and testimony from U.S. officials in support of the act.

White House: USA PATRIOT Act (www.whitehouse.gov/infocus /patriotact). This official White House page for the USA PATRIOT Act focuses on the history of the act. It contains links to key speeches made by the president about the Patriot Act.

Index

Picture Credits

Maury Aaseng, 58–59
AP Images, 27, 38, 48, 56, 65, 71, 79
CBS/Landov, 116
Ken Cedeno/Bloomberg News/Landov, 93
Chao Soi Cheong/AP Images, 8
Kevin Dietsch/UPI/Landov, 41
© Chad Ehlers/Alamy, 85
Stephen Jaffe/AFP/Getty Images, 21
Karen Kasmauski/Science Faction/Getty Images, 100
© Ei Katsumata/Alamy, 82
Spencer Platt/Getty Images, 11
© 2005 Andy Singer and PoliticalCartoons.com, 35
© 2005 John Trever, *The Albuquerque Journal*, and Political
    Cartoons.com, 43
© 2007 John Trever, *The Albuquerque Journal,* and Political
    Cartoons.com, 72
© 2006 Bob Englehart, *The Hartford Courant*, and Political
    Cartoons.com, 87
© Bill Varie /Alamy, 14
Roger L. Wollenberg/UPI/Landov, 9, 34
Alex Wong/Getty Images, 109
Steve Zmina, 15, 29, 51, 103, 107, 115

DATE DUE